T0182491

For Katia and Spritz

DRINK & THINK
VENICE

The Story of Venice in Twenty-Six Bars and Cafés

or

A Counterblast against
too Sober an Inspection of Monuments

Robin Saikia

SOMERSET • LONDON

Drink & Think Venice
1st edition

Published by Blue Guides Limited, a Somerset Books Company
Unit 2, Old Brewery Road, Wiveliscombe, Somerset TA4 2PW
www.blueguides.com. 'Blue Guide' is a registered trademark.

ISBN 978-1-905131-97-6

The author and publisher have made reasonable efforts to ensure the
accuracy of all the information in this book; however, they can accept
no responsibility for any loss, injury or inconvenience sustained by any
traveller as a result of information or advice contained in the guide.

Every effort has been made to trace the copyright owners of material
reproduced in this guide. We would be pleased to hear from any copyright
owners we have been unable to reach.

Statement of editorial independence: Blue Guides, their authors and editors,
are prohibited from accepting payment from any restaurant, hotel or other
establishment for its inclusion in this guide or on blueguides.com, or for a
more favourable mention than would otherwise have been made.

We welcome reader comments and feedback: editorial@blueguides.com.

Cover: iStock © Leafedge; and Imre Bába.

Printed and bound in Hungary by Dürer Nyomda Kft., Gyula.

Contents

Foreword

On a chilly night in January, I found myself wandering the back streets of Venice in search of a suitable subtitle for this book. It was after midnight when I came into a pitch-black *sotoportego*, illuminated only by the electric candle of a wayside shrine and by the ember of my cigar. I fancied I met the shade of the English traveller, Thomas Coryat, whose accounts of Venice in 1608 give us such an immediate and lively impression of what life was like then, in this most improbable of cities. Shaken by the apparition, I reached for my hip flask, charged as always with Poli's exquisite, honey-scented grappa. But I need not have feared. Coryat seemed to applaud the philosophy of my book, saying that he thought it 'A Counterblast Against Too Sober An Inspection Of Monuments'. This is precisely what I hope it is, and certainly what I had set out to achieve. I make no apologies for the frequently subjective and at times opinionated thoughts set out in these pages. They are the fruit of nearly half a century of drinking and thinking in Venice and I hope they will encourage travellers to meditate, as I have done, on the less obvious connections one might make between time and place, past and present. I should add that Coryat's ghost had definitely loaded 'Too Sober

An Inspection' with a double meaning: it suggests that sometimes we are too earnest in our approach to cultural tourism, seeing it as a duty to be performed, a box to be ticked. I suggest that much can be missed if one adopts that approach, and I hope that my book will encourage a fresher, relaxed and more expansive way of looking at things and people. I also firmly believe that the enjoyment of 'culture' can be enhanced by one or more drinks along the way.

Robin Saikia. Venice, 2024

1. TRATTORIA SAN BASILIO

Trattoria San Basilio is a modest, friendly restaurant on the Zattere, by the San Basilio vaporetto stop. One can simply order a drink and sit at one of the few tables outside and over the years I have come to treat it as somewhere to recover from the chore of a weekly shop at the nearby supermarket. A restorative drink, usually taken late on a Friday afternoon, has become something of a ritual and every time I go to Trattoria San Basilio I raise my glass to Air Marshal Robert 'Pussy' Foster of the RAF. I believe there is a strong case for saying that had it not been for Pussy, there would not be a Venice at all—at least not in the form we know it: following the Allied air strike on the German naval base in Venice, which he masterminded in 1945 and which was carefully designed to leave the city unscathed, Pussy may justly be remembered as one of Venice's leading benefactors. Trattoria San Basilio is at the epicentre of where the raid took place, so makes an appropriate place to drink to its success—and in the Air Marshal's honour a circle of admirers has bestowed the nickname 'Pussy's' on the *trattoria*. But who was 'Pussy' and why was his bombardment such a key event?

Trattoria San Basilio.

Pussy Foster christened the raid 'Operation Bowler', entrusting the bombardment to Group Captain George Westlake of the RAF. He told Westlake that if Venice's buildings were to sustain the slightest damage, the culprit would be 'bowler-hatted', meaning relieved of active duty and returned to a mundane desk job. Operation Bowler was among the earliest examples of what we now call a 'surgical strike', an attack designed to destroy only a legitimate military target, causing minimal damage to surrounding buildings and civilians.

Foster was a veteran airman who had served in the Royal Flying Corps in the First World War. He had been a brilliant scholar at Winchester College, where his contemporaries remembered him as a cheerful boy with ruddy cheeks and a mop of blond hair. He wore a permanent smile, somewhat like that of the Cheshire Cat, and it earned him the nickname 'Pussy' among his brother officers. The moniker stuck, as enduring as the smile. Pussy's good nature was balanced by steel and dash. An acknowledged air ace in the First World War, he was also an accomplished linguist. This stood him in good stead when he force-landed in Waziristan in 1923, while serving with 20 Squadron RAF during the Afghan invasion of the Northwest Frontier. Though his badly-damaged plane was immediately surrounded by local tribesmen, Pussy maintained his *sang froid*. He stepped coolly out of the wreckage, beaming good-naturedly. 'Shabash!'

he said, which roughly translates from Urdu as 'Jolly good show!' This endeared him to his captors, who took him back to their camp for a round of feasting and celebration.

In the Second World War, as Air Vice-Marshal, Foster faced an urgent challenge as the Italian Campaign progressed and the Allies fought their way up through Italy. Despite the well-documented miseries of Nazi occupation, Venice had enjoyed a charmed war in comparison to many other regions of Italy. The ancient city of Messina in Sicily had been reduced to rubble. Entire districts of Rome were bombed out of recognition. One of the worst instances was the battle of Monte Cassino, when the Allies blew up the centuries-old monastery, founded by St Benedict. It had been thought to be a key German stronghold but little if any territorial advantage was gained by its annihilation. Since then the Allied high command had been anxious to avoid further unnecessary destruction. This was laudable in theory, but difficult to stick to in practice.

During the course of the campaign the Allies and Italian partisans had inflicted irreversible damage on Italy's road and railway networks, paralysing German supply lines. In the Veneto, the Germans were forced to rely on the network of waterways, shipping arms and supplies into Venice and then inland via the Brenta Canal and its tributaries. It became clear that Venice was every bit as strategically important as Trieste. Trieste might well have been the bridgehead to

Trattoria San Basilio.

central Europe but, for the occupying Germans, Venice remained the gateway to the Italian peninsula. The Allies needed to attack in short order and attempt to cut off the supply line once and for all, simultaneously avoiding a repeat performance of Monte Cassino.

Rising to the challenge, Pussy initiated the raid on 21st March 1945. He began by ordering Group Captain George Westlake to strafe the anti-aircraft emplacements on the Lido and Sant'Erasmo. When these had been knocked out, Westlake led 237 Wing, composed of British, American,

Australian and New Zealand airmen, in towards Venice. They flew in at 10,000 feet in tight formation, west over the Lido, crossing the Giudecca. Westlake was in the lead and when he coolly gave the order, the squadron pulled into a near-vertical dive, heading straight for the German naval installation in the harbour. There was a wail of engines as they sped down towards the target. Below, on the quay, scores of terrified German personnel scattered for cover. Perilously vulnerable but determined to enjoy the '*spettacolo*', Italian families gathered on the rooftops to cheer on the Allied aircraft. They were not disappointed. At 300 feet, when Westlake gave the critical command, 'Bombs away!' and the squadron released its 250-ton payload, the result was spectacular.

A 300-foot crater was blown on the Santa Marta dockside. Two merchant ships and a large cargo vessel were seriously damaged, as were five of the port warehouses. A munitions warehouse containing the German stockpile was completely destroyed, as was a top-secret underwater training school for U-boat personnel. This was an added bonus, since Allied Intelligence had not been aware of it prior to the raid. While the city itself suffered minimal damage, the German naval installation in Venice had taken a pounding from which it could not recover. The port of Venice was completely paralysed and of no use to the Axis forces when the Allied spring offensive against the Gothic

A bottle of Tai, at Trattoria San Basilio.

Line began two weeks later. It is safe to assume that back at HQ at Cesena, Pussy's habitual smile broadened still further. Nobody on the mission was 'bowler-hatted'.

Sadly, despite Pussy's meticulous planning, twenty-nine Venetians died in the raid and a further casualty died of his injuries some years later. They are commemorated in a simple monument on the Fondamenta Santa Marta, where to this day, every year on the anniversary of the raid, a service of remembrance is conducted by the parish priest of Sant'Angelo Raffaele. When I raise my glass at San Basilio, I drink to the Venetians who lost their lives as well as to Pussy Foster.

The owners of Trattoria San Basilio are proud of their white wines and my drink of choice here is Tai, a light dry white wine made in northeast Italy from the Sauvignonasse grape. The wine was known as Tocai until 2008, when the European courts upheld an objection from Hungarian viticulturists, who challenged the right of their Italian counterparts to describe this wine as a 'Tocai', considering the name too similar to Tokaj, the rich and complex Hungarian dessert wine made chiefly from Furmint and Hárslevelű grapes. The names might be similar; the wines are entirely different. The Italians, however, now call their wine Tai when it comes from the Veneto, and Friulano when it comes from Friuli. The Tai at Pussy's has a delicate scent and a pleasing colour, a kind of pale, polished-golden yellow that looks well in the late afternoon Venetian sunlight.

2. HARRY'S BAR

Harry's Bar on Calle Vallaresso is very famous and much copied—with precarious degrees of success—all over the world. It astonishes most first-time visitors by its utter simplicity and absence of flash. The tables and chairs, the crockery and glassware, the panelling on the walls, the light fittings, all have the air of having been there forever. Nothing is showy or obviously expensive. The main room is completely devoid of any of the bourgeois clutter we all know and many of us secretly love. No acres of Fortuny curtains, no nests of Bevilacqua cushions bursting with rare goose down, no venal reliquarium crammed with gaudy *veneziana* in the form of ormolu lions or Murano decanters. Everything is resolutely simple, from the honey-coloured wooden panelling to the crisp white napery and understated cutlery and glassware—indeed the plates, glasses and eating irons were specially designed by Giuseppe Cipriani, the founder of the bar and father of the present owner, Arrigo Cipriani. The simple settings are intended to put guests at their ease. There should be no nervous negotiation of fussy fish knives

or intimidating dessert forks, no agony over which flute for this or what tumbler for that. As to décor, the far wall facing the door bears a simple but noble panorama photo of the lagoon and little more. I can think of few rooms in Europe that proclaim such carefully studied lack of pretension. The harmonious absence of distraction gives one ample space to commune with the spirits of bygone famous regulars— Ernest Hemingway, Coco Chanel, Truman Capote, Charlie Chaplin—as well as numberless nameless heroes such as the Venetian Jews whom Giuseppe Cipriani welcomed during the Nazi occupation, or the partisans who had in him a friend and provider of refuge. This is where the true value of this excellent bar lies, the opportunity it affords for a valuable communion with the alternately uplifting and unsettling episodes of its fascinating past.

Harry's is ever-popular at lunchtime and visitors to Venice have begun treating it as a restaurant rather than as a place to drink, so to be sure of a seat at the bar or at one of the tables, it is advisable to clock in at around 11:30am. My favourite cocktail here is a simple but superb vodka Martini. Devotees have nicknamed this the Chester Kallman, an allusion to W.H. Auden's lover, whose afternoon ritual in New York was to chill glasses in the freezer in preparation for an evening's bibulous symposium. The glasses are chilled in Harry's too and it is not unusual for an attentive barman, having noticed one's clumsy fingerprints on the frosty surface, deftly to

Vodka Martini, at Harry's Bar.

VODKA MARTINI

Ingredients: Vodka, dry vermouth.

Method: Begin with well chilled ingredients.
Sprinkle a dash of vermouth into a mixing glass.
Add a generous measure of
chilled vodka. Stir together. Pour
the mix into a plain, pre-frosted
tumbler. *Eccoci qua!*

decant the remains of the Martini into a freshly wintry glass, often topping it up on the way. One sunny May morning, I took myself to Harry's for a drink to mark the Feast of the Ascension, a central event in the Venetian liturgical calendar that features an exciting regatta as well as a (somewhat corporate) replication of the Marriage of the Doge to the Sea. I was halfway through my topped-up Martini when a burly character burst his way through the swing doors.

He ordered a beer.

But beer is not served in Harry's. Another problem to test the legendary diplomacy of Arrigo Cipriani's staff was that the new guest's shorts, flip-flops and T-shirt were in contravention of the dress code. We all watched Franco, the head barman, quickly weighing up which problem to address first. He chose the dress code. The new guest contended that if he was going to pay these prices his money was as good as anyone's and it didn't matter what he was wearing. But Franco was immovable. Angry and aggrieved, the newcomer turned to go. His parting shot, before he went, was memorable:

'I hate this city.'

I recalled a *graffito* I had first seen ten years ago, on the little stone bridge that takes you from Campo Santa Margherita to the *calle* leading to Piazzale Roma. Five words were stencilled in black spraypaint on the marble balustrade, so indelibly that over a decade's worth of scrubbing has not sufficed to remove them and the slogan is still legible: 'I want my money back.'

There are many people who are disappointed with Venice. What precisely it is they are expecting and what eventually proves to disappoint them would make a book in itself. There was an awkward silence in Harry's for no more than fifteen or twenty seconds after the disgruntled guest departed. To go back to Auden, and to adapt a poem of his, 'Musée des Beaux Arts', the drinkers saw something amazing, a man in shorts falling out of the sky, but there were Bellinis and Martinis to be drunk, and the ship of the moment plied resolutely on.

But are Harry's prices, at 25 or 30 euros a cocktail, too high? The bar is no more expensive than any of its rivals in San Marco (Palazzo Gritti, Florian, Quadri), yet it seems more than anywhere else to trigger the age-old debate over price and value. A quick trawl through the fervid waters of Tripadvisor's low-star reviews reveals any number of raging Calibans. Do they feel short-changed because Harry's does not live up to the shimmering Vegas Venice of their imagination? Because it does not spend the money it takes from customers on decking itself out in reassuringly ostentatious schlock? There are so many ways of incinerating hard-earned money in the pursuit of transitory gratification. One might as well focus one's attention on begetting a memory worth enshrining, rather than the waking nightmare of a mediocre experience one would rather forget. I personally have no problem with the tariff and indeed sometimes feel as though I am complicit in robbing Arrigo, or at least in allowing him to sell himself short. Lord Norwich once observed that Venice ought to be more difficult to get to. I would say that the Harry's drinks menu should be at least double the price of what it is. Both it and the Bar Longhi at the Gritti Palace surely represent the best value in town for superbly-made high-end drinks in unimpeachable settings. Some people will always complain, of course. But Arrigo Cipriani, among his many other unusual accomplishments, holds a black belt in karate.

3. SCHIAVI

As the heat of the day begins to wane in Venice, the minds of many turn to the idea of an *aperitivo*, which traditionally comes in the form of a small glass of wine known as an *ombra*, or 'shadow'. The history of the *ombra* is well known. In the old days, wine vendors in Piazza San Marco would move their pitches as the day wore on, following the immense, cool shade of the Campanile as it moved across the square. Thus for drinkers, the Piazza became an enormous sundial, measuring out life and drinks, increment by increment, until dusk fell. Today there are no itinerant wine merchants in the Piazza and that area of Venice is geared to a different clientèle. Nonetheless, the *ombra* persists throughout the city in general, as a cut-price drink that usually comes in one of three forms. First, in one of the few remaining old-school *bàcari*, one might be served *vino sfuso* ('wine in bulk'), piped directly into one's glass from a vast demijohn supplied from a smallholding on the mainland by one of the proprietor's relatives; second, the bar might dispense its house wine from a plump, two-litre bottle, topping this up from time to time from a demijohn at the back of the shop; third, one might order *bianco* or *rosso* '*alla spina*', on draught, from a pump. While many disparage the quality of these draught wines, they are pretty good for what they are—and for the price, they are excellent.

If there is an ultimate place to take an *ombra*, it might well be Schiavi, the popular bar and wine merchant on the Fondamenta Nani in Dorsoduro. They sell the finest wine and spirits that the Veneto—and indeed Italy—can offer, but their house Pinot Nero is favoured by the locals and given away at a euro a beaker. My drink of choice here, though, is not Pinot Nero but a rosé, a Bardolino Chiaretto, a cheerful wine with an ancient and distinguished lineage dating back to the viticulture of ancient Greece and Rome. We owe its present Italian incarnation to the Venetian historian, politician and senator Pompeo Molmenti who, in the last decade of the 19th century, pioneered the revival of a process that had been popular around Lake Garda since the Roman occupation of Cisalpine Gaul. The basic and time-honoured principle of Chiaretto, as with all traditional rosé wines, is to allow the juice from your pressed grapes only minimal contact with the grape skins—a few hours at most, hence the expression *vino di una notte*, a 'wine of one night'. That way, the resulting vintage assumes the gentle translucence of a pink topaz, rather than deepening into the dark rubies and carnelians one sees in red wines.

Chiaretto is the ideal accompaniment for *cicchetti*, the

Schiavi.

simple but famous savoury snacks served in most if not all Venetian bars. Alessandra De Respinis, 'Sandra', the chatelaine of Schiavi, is rightly regarded as the high priestess of *cicchetti*, and has written an entertaining and informative recipe book about them. The central philosophy, if there is one, might lie in the interesting collision of tastes that make up many of the recipes. I might order a feisty gorgonzola paired with a delicate apricot jam, for instance, or salty anchovies offset by comforting slices of hard-boiled egg. The holy grail of *cicchetti*, though, is *baccalà mantecato*, stockfish slowly cooked with bay leaves and lemon juice and then beaten into a delicate 'butter' and spread on crisp, fresh bread or feather-light polenta.

But how does an Atlantic fish come to be so popular in Adriatic Venice? As I tuck into Sandra's *baccalà*, I raise a glass of Chiaretto to the memory of Pietro Querini, the 15th-century Venetian merchant seaman who found himself blown hideously off course during a voyage to from Crete to Bruges in 1432. Shipwrecked off the coast of Norway, he and the eleven members of his crew who survived were rescued and looked after by fishermen at Røst in the Lofoten Islands, with whom they stayed for three months. Querini was much taken with the simple good manners and good looks of the people and was especially interested in the method they employed for drying stockfish, a method he eventually brought home to Venice and the Veneto. His

the patron saints of haymakers, whose names are also jointly invoked for the detection of thieves. Inside the church, in the Chapel of the Holy Sacrament, is one of many versions that Tintoretto painted of the *Last Supper*.

There was a time when I imagined this early work to be one of the more festive renditions of the conventionally sombre gathering. The Son of Man himself is portrayed in relatively good spirits, the whole *mise-en-scène* reminiscent of a drinking party in a spit-and-sawdust *bàcaro*. Indeed one of the Disciples, with his back to us, strongly reinforces this perception. He seems to be only half-listening to what Jesus is saying, so intent is he on reaching for a large demijohn in order to refill his already half-full glass of very delicate pink wine. Is this an earlier incarnation of Chiaretto, perhaps the favoured tipple of Tintoretto, his studio assistants and models? But then Ruskin awakened me to a darker reading of the painting: 'There is singular baseness,' he tells us, 'in the circumstance that one of the near Apostles, while all the others are...intent upon Christ's words, "One of you shall betray me," is going to help himself to wine out of a bottle which stands behind him. In so doing he stoops towards the table, the flask being on the floor. If intended for the action of Judas at this moment, there is the painter's usual originality in the thought...' Judas this must be, so shocked by the Master's revelation that instinctively, to give himself Dutch courage, he grasps for the nearest bottle. Perhaps

Tintoretto, *Last Supper* (1560s),
with its glass of delicate pink wine.

nowhere else in art is the phrase *in vino veritas* endowed
with such unusual resonance. As I reach for my beaker of
Chiaretto, I raise it to Querini and to Tintoretto.

4. CAFFÈ QUADRI

G ran Caffè Quadri in Piazza San Marco was founded by Giorgio Quadri and his Greek wife, Naxina, in 1775. Their idea was to create the perfect coffee shop, in an attempt to expand the steady—though by no means dramatic—local enthusiasm for the drink that had been introduced by Turkish merchants in 1683.

Coffee, or *acqua negra bollente* ('boiling black water') as it was called in Quadri's time, is now central to Italian life, so I find it pleasing to sit in the Piazza from time to time and enjoy an *espresso*, which at Quadri amounts to rather more than the boiling black water one might expect at less opulent bars. The coffee is supplied by the Laboratorio di Torrefazione Giamaica Caffè in Verona, an epicurean roastery presided over by Maestro Gianni Frasi. Having first obtained his beans in person from what Quadri dramatically describes as an 'undisclosed location in the Indonesian archipelago', Maestro Frasi brings them back to Verona. There he roasts them in a vintage coffee-roaster, a handsome chunk of Italian industrial chic manufactured in the 1950s. It is said that only Frasi can judge the precise moment at which to suspend the roast, capturing the richness and depth of flavour one hunts for in a good *espresso*.

Over time, Quadri accumulated a diversity of devoted regulars, among them Byron, Stendhal, Proust, Wagner, Mikhail Gorbachev, François Mitterand and Woody Allen. But when I go to Quadri I routinely toast the memory of a less well-known adopted son of Venice: Jacopo Calascione, the civic bandmaster in the late 19th and early 20th centuries. Whenever I toast him, I always meditate on his chance meeting with Wagner here, and the understated but significant part he played in popularising Wagner's music in the city.

The 1882 *Parsifal* at the Festspielhaus in Bayreuth was a valedictory flourish for Wagner, who was by then ageing and ill. Perhaps he sensed it; during the final performance, at the beginning of the last act, he came quietly into the pit and took the baton from Hermann Levi. It was to be Wagner's last appearance as composer-conductor. At the end of the opera season he decided to winter in Venice, for health reasons— perhaps an odd choice given the notoriously chilly climate here. However, it was the logical place to go, since in April that year he had already rented a floor of Palazzo Vendramin Calergi from its then owner, Count Bardi, and had spent the late spring and early summer putting the finishing touches to *Parsifal*.

It should be said that although Wagner's sojourns

4. CAFFÈ QUADRI

in Venice were few and short (he was never a long-term resident), this has never prevented Venetians from claiming him as an adopted son. Sometimes they are criticised for 'cheating' in this regard, but if you ever hear that said, you can always reply that Wagner refashioned the gondolier's classic warning cry, '*Oè!*', into Siegfried's leitmotif horn-call. That alone is surely sufficient to merit posthumously awarding him the keys of the city.

During his 1882 visit, on 21st April, Wagner heard the civic band performing the duet from *Rigoletto* in one of their afternoon concerts in Piazza San Marco. He introduced himself to the bandmaster, Jacopo Calascione, a stout, stalwart Sicilian of medium height and military bearing, who sported splendid handlebar moustaches and a clutch of medals. Calascione had been a familiar sight in Piazza San Marco since his appointment in the late 1870s. Every afternoon he would march his band into the square and perform medleys of Italian favourites: Verdi, Puccini, Donizetti, Rossini. Moreover, Calascione was no ordinary civic bandmaster, but a dedicated and well-informed Wagnerian who introduced a number of his own Wagner arrangements into the afternoon programmes.

On this occasion, Wagner congratulated him on the splendid rendition of Verdi's duet, asking if the band might play him their arrangement of the Sinfonia from Rossini's *Gazza Ladra*. Calascione promptly had the score sent over.

The meeting was afterwards reported in the *Gazzettino*, the local paper, and the band were proud of Wagner's praise, since he was known to be an irascible critic.

On his return to Venice later that year, after Bayreuth, Wagner met Calascione again, this time by invitation. The maestro wrote to him saying the band would be honoured if he were to attend their performance of a pot-pourri of arrangements from *Lohengrin*, to be given on 5th November. This was a bold move. Wagner invited Calascione to his *palazzo* the next day. The meeting began well enough, with Wagner warmly praising Calascione's interpretation in general. However, he soon launched into a lecture, observing that the *tempo* Calascione took in Elsa and Ortrud's duet was a little too rushed, particularly in the *stretta*. The episode gives a fair taste of what it must have been like to be on the receiving end of Wagner's rigorous aesthetic discourse. Calascione, by way of excuse, made the fatal (and very Italian) mistake of referring to his *fuoco sacro*, the 'sacred fire' that burns in the heart of every sensitive musician and conductor.

'That fire! That fire!' cried Wagner. 'Water, more like! All these people boast of this *sacro fuoco*, and on that pretext they interpret the music contrary to the composer's intentions. That fire! It is the composer who determines when the *fuoco* should happen, when the situation requires it, when the dramatic moment calls for it!'

The successors of Jacopo Calascione, performing outside Caffè Quadri.

Despite this rocky disagreement, the two men parted on good terms. This, so far as we know, was the last time they met. Wagner died in Venice on 13th February 1883.

Calascione benefited enormously from the inauguration of the annual Wagner commemorations in Venice from 1902 onwards. But as well as being a great Wagnerian, he was also a dedicated servant of his adopted city. When the Campanile of San Marco collapsed, also in 1902, there was Calascione in the months that followed, resolutely performing fundraising concerts in aid of the rebuilding programme. Sadly, his career came to an abrupt end on a bright afternoon in the early autumn of 1907. As an expectant crowd awaited, the 67-year-old hero marched his band into Piazza San Marco for the last time. As they struck up a number from *Rigoletto*, he swayed slightly, sank to his knees, and collapsed. A sudden, fatal heart attack. It was no surprise to learn that thousands attended his funeral parade later that year—and that his *fuoco sacro* still burns bright in the annals of Venice.

5. VILLA LAGUNA

The Hotel Villa Laguna on the Venice Lido has a terrace bar looking out towards San Marco. The hotel itself is an interesting building, its pitched roof, decorative detailing and markedly alpine feel making perfect sense when one realises it was once a Habsburg holiday chalet. It belongs in the Viennese tradition one sees elsewhere on the Lido, a happy legacy of the Austrian occupation. This air of quiet elegance makes Villa Laguna a perfect place to watch the sun go down and enjoy Venice's traditional apéritif, the Spritz. On a clear evening, it is easy to recall Shelley's lines on the Venetian sunset, as 'if the Earth and Sea had been dissolved into one lake of fire'. For a few precious moments one can see Venice as he and Byron once saw it:

'...from their many isles, in evening's gleam,
Its temples and its palaces did seem
Like fabrics of enchantment pil'd to Heaven.'

The story of Spritz is well documented, often repeated on bar menus and in hotel brochures. To summarise very

'As if the Earth and Sea had been dissolved into one lake of fire...' The view from Villa Laguna.

Aperol, Cynar, Select, Campari. The four main liqueurs from which Venetian Spritz is made, seen here lined up on the bar of the Hotel Canal Grande in the *sestiere* of Santa Croce.

briefly, during the Austrian occupation of Venice from 1815, it became clear that the occupying troops were unused to drinking wine and became drunk alarmingly quickly. Their wine rations were suitably watered and discipline was adequately enough restored. As time went on, with the invention of carbonated water and the manufacture of ever more alluring aperitif liqueurs, the Spritz as we know it was born. There are many hybrid versions (on the wall in La Palanca, a simple bar-restaurant on the Giudecca, there is a humorous encyclopaedic list), but the four leaders are as follows: Spritz Bitter (made with Campari), Spritz Aperol (made with the bright orange liqueur of that name), Spritz Cynar and Spritz Select. The recipe is always as follows: first Prosecco, then the liqueur, then soda water, measured in equal proportions; then ice; then a slice of lemon or orange, their thickness and freshness dictated by the generosity

Spritz Select, Spritz Campari and Spritz Aperol, side by side at Da Gino in the *sestiere* of Dorsoduro.

The bar at Villa Laguna with bottles of Campari (top shelf left), Select (centre) and Aperol (right) prominently displayed.

or parsimony of the proprietor. My advice is to insist on lemon in Aperol, to offset the cloying sweetness, and orange in Campari, to soften the bitterness. As with many cocktails, there is a dangerous tendency towards gratuitous experimentation with a Spritz. I have suffered both sake and absinthe as ill-judged alternatives to the stock liqueurs. The variable results underline an old maxim, as applicable to drinks as it is to life in general: namely, that just because something can be done, doesn't necessarily mean that it should be. One interesting variant worth considering, however, is the use of a still wine, say a basic Pinot Grigio, in preference to Prosecco. This can lend a depth and gravity to the drink that works well in the meditative seasons of autumn and winter, when one's optimistic springtime fizz has temporarily lost its bubbles.

In my early days in Venice I quickly realised that Aperol was too sweet for my taste and for many years I drank the Campari version. I had always been captivated by the huge illuminated letters, CAMPARI, that one would see glassily shimmering against the night sky on the *vaporetto* ride to the Lido. Sadly, these were taken down some years ago, though they still endure in the mind's eye and shine brightly in my dreams, an emblem of happy times spent in nightclubs and on the beach. Campari is said to be a sure safeguard against malaria, on account of its quinine content. One evening, on the terrace of the Excelsior, in the midst of a particularly trying raid by a squadron of mosquitos, I heard an elderly gentleman saying just this to his wife. But once one senses that a festive drink is a medicine in disguise, the joy is gone—and if this is true of Campari, it must be doubly so of Cynar. Cynar is made from artichokes, which though I like well enough are not really a fit foundation for an agreeable beverage. For me, Cynar belongs to that pseudo-medicinal family of drinks comprised of pick-me-ups such as Jägermeister, Underberg, Ramazzotti, Fernet Branca and Gammel Dansk. Substances to be taken furtively,

Spritz Select at Villa Laguna, with a view of San Lazzaro degli Armeni, the island where Byron stayed.

at a single swallow; sly sharpeners designed to vanquish the crapula and set one on the road without censure from stern onlookers. Little more, in other words, than a shifty but effective hangover cure. For purely recreational drinking it has to be ruled out.

So I was left with Spritz Select. Select, as a liqueur, is unimpeachably Venetian, having been invented in the twenties in the *sestiere* of Castello by the Pilla family, who sought to capitalise on the post-war hedonism of the period. Thirty botanicals, including rhubarb root and juniper, are carefully blended and macerated, the manufacturers tell us, to give structure and persistence. These qualities are easily analysed; Select happily combines the best aspects of sugary Aperol and bitter Campari, and it is this that gives it its winning quality. To borrow an expression from Alexander Pope, it has an 'easy vigour'. I have drunk Spritz Select happily now for over a decade but it was only recently, during an idle investigation of how this quartet of Spritzes have been marketed over the last century, that I came to realise how happy my choice was.

In the thirties, a popular Aperol poster featured a young woman gazing adoringly into her boyfriend's eyes as they toasted one another, a bottle of Aperol placed prominently in

SPRITZ SELECT

Ingredients: 2 parts Select, 3 parts Prosecco, 1 part soda water.

Method: Pour the Select into a stemmed glass on top of a few cubes of ice. Add the Prosecco and then the soda. Garnish with a slice of lemon.

the foreground. An improvement perhaps on earlier attempts, conceived in the twenties to attract female drinkers: *Signora! L'Aperol mantiene la linea!* 'Madam! Aperol keeps your figure trim!' By the fifties the air of happy-go-lucky girlsomeness was further enhanced by a poster showing a young woman perched happily on the pillion of her beau's Vespa. The couple sped not along a rural lane in the Veneto nor along the Via Sandro Gallo on the Lido, but instead across an azure, early evening sky, leaving, unaccountably, a trail of ox-eye daisies in their wake. Among recent, cinematic, advertisements for Aperol, a young woman is seen sliding exuberantly down the balustrade of a grand helical staircase, to join a throng of revellers dancing the night away in the atrium below. I can think of myself only as a genial bystander in such scenes, rather than a fully committed participant.

As to Cynar, my medicinal prejudices were underpinned on discovering that it had been marketed as a health drink— no surprise, given the reputation of the artichoke among nutritionists. The fifties' advertising agencies were tasked with glamorising the nutritional qualities of Cynar and they did not disappoint. In one poster, a young skier at the peak of physical prowess soars above us, the accompanying text proclaiming that the 'artichoke is health' and that drinking Cynar will leave us *pronti a godere le gioie di un'esistenza piena e felice*, 'ready to embrace the joys of a full and happy life'. None of these campaigns were sufficient to turn me away from Select. I was gratified to see the ad men's conception of the 'Select' man, when I finally came across it. A poster from the early forties shows a man in early middle age (or possibly in very late youth; the artist has cleverly left this open to interpretation), offering a sort of *media via* Dorian Gray. He gazes appreciatively at an exquisite glass he holds aloft in his right hand, his smile suggesting an individual at ease with the world, one who has placed himself at a decent though not untraversable distance from the hurly-burly of the *dolce vita*. He is now content to savour his Select in, say, the agreeable confines of an elegant *palazzetto*, or a Liberty villa on the Lido. Select, as the old sales puff had it, is 'the aperitif of the connoisseur'.

6. IL MERCANTE

Il Mercante is an elegant cocktail bar directly opposite the façade of Santa Maria Gloriosa dei Frari, just across the little *rio*. Under its red canvas awning it still preserves the name of its former incarnation, the Caffè dei Frari O. Toppo, a famous and much-loved coffee house founded in 1870. The new owners have taken care to preserve key elements of the old Belle Époque interior, so the arrangements are still as pleasing as they used to be in the old days, especially thanks to the swish old staircase leading to the mezzanine. The new cocktail bar is very forward-looking—indeed whenever I scan the innovative list I feel sure the shade of the Futurist poet Filippo Tommaso Marinetti must have had a hand in it: a preoccupation with creating new and startling pairings of food and drink, as part of a general drive toward overturning the old world, was a fascinating Futurist sideline. Thankfully, Il Mercante does not go quite as far as Marinetti did in his 1935 masterpiece, *La Cucina Futuristica*, in which he proposes such unsettling combinations as steak in Eau de Cologne. Nonetheless the Mercante cocktail list, beautifully designed and illustrated,

An artisanal cocktail from Il Mercante's ever-evolving list.

is a poem in itself, cleverly stimulating one's curiosity. The menu changes regularly, as the bartenders strive for ever more exotic innovations, but the cocktails are always excellent and never disappoint. Last time I was there I was offered 'Three Apples of Concord', 'Seven Witches' and 'Saint

Nicholas of the Lettuce'. The cocktail I chose was 'L'Orto di Venezia'. Although the English translation, 'Venetian Vegetable Garden', may not seem particularly promising, the drink was exceptionally good and unimpeachably Venetian in feel: gin infused with Violetto artichokes from the market gardens of Sant'Erasmo, elderflower wine, and finally—a brave and pleasing touch—sea water.

When I come to Il Mercante, it is usually after paying a visit to the church of the Frari. Visitors typically come here to marvel at Titian's *Assumption* and his *Pesaro Madonna*, and at Giovanni Bellini's great triptych, *The Virgin with Saints Nicholas of Bari, Peter, Mark and Benedict*. What draws me more than any of these, though, are its sculptures. If one needed to reach for a spectacular example of the vital—if not downright theatrical—qualities inherent in marble, then the Frari monument to Antonio Canova is one of the finest examples in Europe.

Antonio Canova (1757–1822) was a child prodigy, born into a family of stonecutters and stonemasons in Possagno, a small town in the Veneto some forty miles northwest of Venice. His boyhood precocity was later enshrined in an elaborate and tantalisingly plausible painting made in 1885 by an American artist, Pinckney Marcius-Simons, entitled *The Child Canova Modelling a Lion out of Butter*. The unverified story goes that the enterprising ten-year-old was called in to replace a broken Murano glass centrepiece made for a dinner party given by Senator Giovanni Falier. What is certainly true is that Canova was a boy genius, brought up by his paternal grandfather, who set him to work as an apprentice and later sent him to the Accademia di Belli Arte in Venice, where he won a clutch of prizes. Half a century later, he had become one of the most prominent artists in Europe, with a stellar range of patrons including the Vatican in Rome, the Senate in Venice, the Prince Regent in Britain and Napoleon in France.

As to Napoleon, Venice can be as proud of Canova for his diplomatic activities as they are for his art. In 1815, following the Little Corporal's defeat, Canova was appointed a Minister Plenipotentiary by Pope Pius VII, charged with recovering works of art that had been looted during the Napoleonic occupation of Italy. Among the many pieces whose return he successfully negotiated were the four Horses of St Mark's, which were brought back to the Basilica from Paris in 1816. (The Horses which adorn the façade today are copies; the originals are in the museum inside.)

Canova died in 1822 and his monument, a striking pyramidal structure immediately to one's left as one enters the Frari, was completed by five of his pupils in 1827, working to his designs. Years earlier, in 1794, Canova had completed a preliminary pyramidal design intended as a mausoleum for Titian, but this was rejected as being too *outré* for the Frari and eventually recycled as the monument to Maria Christina of Austria (daughter of Maria Theresa), in the Augustinerkirche in Vienna. The recent restoration of the Frari monument, funded by Venice in Peril, was completed in time for the bicentenary of Canova's death (13th October 2022), a fitting and long-overdue tribute. The heroic undertaking involved the complete dismantling of the enormous monument, slab by slab, followed by a thorough clean of the marble, which for over two centuries had suffered internal bleeding from the corroded iron pins that had held it together. Ancient and faulty drainage systems running around the perimeter of the church had also taken their toll: the monument had become so saturated that several of the statues appeared to be weeping, or sweating. All that is now, thankfully, over.

It is interesting to compare the Vienna and Venice monuments. While the Vienna pyramid comes across as an unusual stand-alone piece, its Venice counterpart has been cleverly woven into the fabric and spirit of the Frari, an outstanding achievement by Canova's pupils. This comes down to a simple feat of choreography. The principal players in the drama are the figures we see going in solemn procession towards the gloomy open gateway of the pyramid. The mourning figures of Sculpture, Painting and Architecture are accompanied by three young attendants bearing blazing torches, symbols of the immortality of the soul. To the left of the gateway, the winged Lion of St

Sculpture, Painting and Architecture process in mourning to the tomb. Monument to Antonio Canova in the church of the Frari.

Mark dozes, his book proclaiming the Evangelist (*Pax Tibi Marce*) for now closed beneath his paws. Immediately to the lion's left, in the foreground, a reclining figure represents the genius of Canova, the torch he holds upturned and extinguished to serve as an emblem of the sculptor's passing. Above the doorway is a bas-relief profile of Canova himself, in a roundel formed by intertwined sculpted snakes, a symbol of immortality. The roundel is supported by a pair of flanking angels. All this taken together might seem not much more than an excellent and imaginative example of neoclassical funerary art. It is not until one chances to view it at the end of Mass—and it is well worth timing a visit accordingly—that Canova's monument becomes something infinitely more than just a static tribute. As the congregation departs, filing out from between the magnificent choir stalls and along the aisle, the worshippers seem to join the sculpted mourners. This theatrical illusion is one of the most striking enactments of *memento mori* I have ever experienced.

7. BLU BAR

In the *sestiere* of Dorsoduro, hard by the little bridge that takes you to the church of San Sebastiano, is the Blu Bar with its Chinese proprietor Mr Chen. There is a simple zinc counter, pumps for dispensing wine or beer, a cabinet of brioches and *tramezzini*, a few tables inside and out—and in one corner, taking up every square inch of available space, a cramped *ridotto* of luridly-themed slot machines. These are played from dawn to dusk, usually by a gathering of middle-aged or elderly Venetian ladies and gentlemen, though occasionally plumbers, dustmen and gondoliers will call in during their lunch break and chance their arm for a few minutes.

There are several Chinese bars in Venice, all nearly identical, but for me Chen's (as we call it) is the Holy Grail. One reason for this is its function as an emblem of Chinese integration into Venetian society. The second is its proximity to San Sebastiano, one of my favourite churches. It is a magnificent monument to the genius of a single individual: nearly everything of note in it, bar Titian's *St Nicholas*, bears the unmistakable signature of Veronese, from the grand cycle of paintings of scenes from The Book of Esther to ancillary details such as the cornices, frames and marble supports made by workmen from meticulous drawings supplied by the artist. The work was undertaken at the time of The Council of Trent, a papal counterblast to the Protestant Reformation, which sought, amongst much else, to overturn Protestant objections to idolatry in art and to re-establish and celebrate the inspirational virtues of religious painting. Legions of artists were pressed into service to achieve this grand objective, and the result might cause one to reflect on an unshakeable truism: that any pictorial strategy of this kind will only be as effective as the artists are truly capable: the pious and sugary work of hosts of indifferent painters served to inflame rather than extinguish the stern dictates of Protestantism. Veronese, however, rose to the occasion with a scheme of immense grandeur and originality.

The drink I invariably choose at Chen's is *caffè corretto*, black coffee 'corrected' with a slug of grappa. Purist devotees of *corretto* may well insist that the grappa is served in a separate glass, so that one might decant it into the empty coffee cup, give it a quick swirl, and down it in one. The fragrant mix of coffee grounds and spirit that results is known as a *rasentìn*, literally a 'rinse' in local dialect—a peculiarly Venetian ritual. *Rasentìn* carries the notion of making a 'clean sweep', perhaps conferring some degree of virtue on the delightfully self-indulgent and somewhat pagan ceremonial.

Veronese's *Triumph of Mordechai* (1555-6), on the ceiling of San Sebastiano.

Coffee, *panini* and Chinese ravioli, on offer at Blu Bar.

One summer evening, as I was standing by the bridge outside the Blu Bar, dealing with a *caffè corretto*, I became aware of an unusual figure standing next to me. He was a Chinese man in his early sixties, slender and elegantly dressed. His silk shirt might have been by Charvet; his suit was Italian (probably Prada); his shoes were unmistakably English. What was he? The local slot machine magnate perhaps, or a broker who had ridden the ebb and flow of the Hang Seng and now owned a chain of nightclubs in

Macao? Or perhaps a retired martial arts actor who had grown quietly rich working on films with Bruce Lee and Chuck Norris. Working on my usual bar-hopping premise, that inside every unassuming individual there may be a fascinating stereotype wildly signalling to be let out, I decided to engage him in conversation. Jimmy was his name. His story turned out to be more prosaic but no less interesting than my fantastical speculations.

The year 2006 saw the publication of *Ho voglia di te*, a romantic novel by the Roman author Federico Moccia. This was later made into a hugely successful film, *I Want You*, directed by Luis Prieto, starring Riccardo Scamarcio and Laura Chiatti. A set piece in the film is the episode where Chiatti and Scamarcio swear their eternal love for one another, inscribing their names on a padlock, which they then cast into the Tiber. This caught the popular imagination, with the result that (to the dismay of civic authorities worldwide) the 'lovelock' became an instant craze. And in a classic case of life failing to imitate art, instead of consigning their lovelocks to the waters as in the film, lovers chose to attach them to bridges, railings and balustrades. Every city from Paris to Peking, from Brooklyn to Bogotá, suffered a massive plague of lovelocks, and unsurprisingly Venice's Accademia Bridge was no exception. As quickly as the authorities harvested the padlocks with bolt-cutters, fresh clusters would appear. It was only after

Lovelocks at Santi Apostoli.

the Comune introduced a system of swingeing fines that the craze was brought to an end—but while it lasted, there was money to be made and Jimmy was one of the first to unlock the income stream.

In addition to bars like Mr Chen's, Venice has a large number of Chinese-run general stores that sell everything from kitchen equipment to watches, dusters, pocket-knives, torches, phone-chargers, souvenirs, Wellington boots and cheap jewellery. Jimmy had for some years owned shares in and financed several of these enterprises. As the lovelock craze gained momentum, he ensured that all his stores were amply equipped—and at between 5 and 10 euros a padlock this proved to be a smart move. Not content to rely solely on a fixed retail platform, Jimmy also made sure that his contacts among the wandering Dravidian rose-sellers and African fake handbag peddlers were also supplied with padlocks. These itinerant vendors would set off at dawn and entice young lovers into the purchase of padlocks. Twice a day Jimmy himself, or one of his henchmen, would meet the agents to collect the spoils. As I remarked to Jimmy, the story is a film in itself. I complimented him on his elegant and agreeably expensive appearance, the result of imagination and industry, saying that I wished more people in Venice could be such an adornment. He thanked me, with a remark that seemed to sum up better than anything the spirit of modern capitalism: 'I always try to give something back.'

The church of San Giacomo dall'Orio
and its polished green 'jewel shaft'.

8. OSTERIA DA FILO

Campo San Giacomo dall'Orio is often missed by visitors, since it cannot be said to be on the way to or from anywhere. It is a resolutely Venetian backwater. The main reason for a visitor to come here is to see the church, with its magnificent ship's-keel roof and some fine paintings, among them Veronese's *St Lawrence between St Jerome and St Prosper*, a curious and faintly comical piece featuring a cherub bearing palm leaves, floating upside down above the assembled saints. But by far the most captivating object in the church, to me at least, is the green stone column in the right-hand transept, a startling vertical brushstroke of unexpected colour amid the cool gold and russet palette of the perpetually dim interior.

I had marvelled at this column as a child, having seen it for the first time after a holiday argument with my mother, about pizza or ice cream, or both. Furious as only a child can be in such circumstances, I found some solace in running my hands over the column's sparkling green surface. And just as one would swear eternal friendship to childhood companions and agree to meet every year at an appointed time and place, so I swore to the column that it would be my friend for life. It is a promise I have kept. It was not until much later that I learned, through Ruskin, that such columns are known as 'jewel shafts'. This one features in Gabriele d'Annunzio's *Il fuoco*, a romantic novel set in Venice. 'Do you know the green column that is in San Giacomo dall'Orio?' asks Daniele, one of the protagonists. 'What a sublime thing it is. It looks like nothing so much as the fossilised condensation of an immense green forest. Tracing its innumerable veins, the eye travels in a dream through a sylvan mystery. While gazing at it, I have visited the woody uplands of Sila and the glades of Hercynia.' In D'Annunzio's vision the column is a petrified relic of a vanished primeval forest. Perhaps it might be said that the whole of Venice rests on such columns. Its *campi* and *palazzi* are, after all, built upon submerged piles of Istrian pine from the forests of the Adriatic coast, which Venice controlled. As one contemplates the breadth and scope of control once exercised by Venice in the Eastern Mediterranean as a whole, one's thoughts inevitably turn to the events of the Fourth Crusade.

The Fourth Crusade of 1202–4 was perhaps the most far-reaching and controversial of the Republic's expansionist projects. The crusade unfolded in a most unusual sequence of events, beginning with the arrival in Venice of the crusading army, composed mostly of Frankish commanders

'Like the fossilised condensation of an immense green forest...While gazing at it, I have visited the woody uplands of Sila and the glades of Hercynia.' Gabriele d'Annunzio.

and their retinues. The original purpose of the crusade was to recapture Jerusalem from the Egyptian Ayyubid Sultanate, Venice's role being to supply a fleet to transport the crusading army. Venice duly built, at breakneck speed, a new fleet fit for purpose, but the army was unable to pay the contracted fees. The Doge, Enrico Dandolo, first held the crusaders hostage on the Lido before finally striking a deal with them that led to a complete abortion of the original Egyptian project. Dandolo first deployed the crusaders to assist him in subduing piracy along the Dalmatian coast; this done, the army was despatched to Constantinople, where it besieged and sacked the city. The atrocities perpetrated were well documented by contemporary observers. The crusaders ran riot for three days, raping women and children and murdering clerics. In Hagia Sophia, the patriarchal cathedral, they smashed the silver iconostasis and set fire to precious manuscripts. In a gruesomely staged tableau, that immediately became a defining moment both for contemporary chroniclers and later historians, a group of crusaders installed a prostitute on the patriarchal throne, forcing her to sing obscene songs while they drank wine from holy vessels. Wholesale looting followed; as much of value as was portable was taken. Venice installed her own puppet ruler on the throne of Byzantium and as a result gained conclusive domination of the eastern Mediterranean and the trade routes it afforded. Much of beauty that one sees and loves in Venice came about as a result of the wealth that flowed into the Republic following the crusade.

Among the most famous trophies brought back to Venice was the Quadriga, the four Horses of St Mark's (or the Horses of the Constantinople Hippodrome, as they might properly be called). We do not know for certain, but the San Giacomo dall'Orio 'jewel shaft' may also have been among the shiploads of loot. It is tempting to imagine its journey from its original site to the docks, where cursing stevedores and their overseers craned it into the hold of a waiting Venetian galley. With it, perhaps, came the pale green font, also made of ancient marble and also in San Giacomo dall'Orio, at the top of the aisle.

I think about all this every time I come to San Giacomo, pondering not for the first time nor the last on the dubious saga of pillage and plunder that underpins the beauty of this city. And as an antidote to it, I choose something truly Venetian as my drink: Prosecco. There are a number of places to enjoy it: the one I make for, when in Campo San Giacomo dall'Orio of an evening, is Da Filo in Calle del Tentor, an *osteria* which doubles as a venue for jazz music on Wednesday nights.

The first recorded use of the word *prosecco* is in a dithyramb, a Dionysian hymn, entitled *Il Roccolo*, published in 1754 by Father Valeriano Canati, a Theatine priest. He anagrammatised his name on the title page to Aureliano Acanti, a somewhat half-hearted attempt to conceal his clerical identity. Prosecco is among the thirty or so Veneto wines celebrated in this curious poem. Canati describes it as being *melaromatico*, 'apple-scented', which is certainly one of the qualities that comes to mind as one sips it today. Its light, slightly sweet acidity is one of its most important characteristics. It is very light, very easy to drink, pale in colour and gentle in terms of alcohol level. But *Il Roccolo* also speaks of Prosecco as a cloudy wine. He must have drunk it *col fondo*, in other words unfiltered and still containing its

sediment. When Prosecco became internationally popular from the late 1970s onwards, the *col fondo* method fell from favour, but today it has caught on again thanks to local viticulturists eager to revive traditional methods. If you can find it, I recommend it. It is known either as Prosecco *col fondo* or *sui lieviti* ('on the lees') and it is a style that predates the *méthode champenoise*. A secondary fermentation takes place in the bottle and the sediment remains. Reliable producers are Gregoletto and Barichel, whose vineyards are in the golden triangle of Prosecco, bounded by Conegliano, Valdobbiadene and Vittorio Veneto. Interestingly, Prosecco made in this way is bottled not with a cork but with a crown cap, the kind of crimped metal closure you find on beer bottles, and this disqualifies it from the DOCG category. But Prosecco *col fondo*, producers insist, is not some funky new-age natural wine. It is the continuation of an ancient heritage.

9. OSTERIA AL SQUERO

Al Squero is a small but busy bar directly opposite the gondola boatyard (*squero*) at San Trovaso, just off the Zattere in Dorsoduro. It has a wonderful selection of *cicchetti* and a useful wine list. I usually drink Soave when I come here. We tend to have dangerous preconceptions about this wine, so often abused as a lukewarm accompaniment to lacklustre gallery openings. But a good Soave, made with organically grown Garganega grapes and served suitably chilled, reminds one what a wonderful wine this can be: its the signature fruitiness offset by a sharp citrus tang. Soave is a true wine of the Veneto, from east of Verona, close to the zone where Valpolicella is grown. The best Soave comes from the higher vineyards and it is not a dainty wine: a true Soave has a chunky, medium body and a heady bouquet.

Once equipped with my wine, and a selection of *cicchetti* on paper plates, I like to stand outside on the *fondamenta*, marvelling at the repairs in train at any given time at the boatyard opposite. One young man, stripped to the waist, energetically applies a fresh coat of inky-black lacquer;

The gondola repair yard on Rio San Trovaso.

another scrapes barnacles off the bright green underside of an upended craft; presently, an old lady emerges muttering from the dim interior of the yard, lambasting a cloud of dust from a plump, ornately-tasselled cushion; a large tabby cat sits motionless by the radio, indifferent to the agreeably retro strains of Adriano Celentano's *Il tempo se ne va*. If you are lucky you might hear one of the craftsmen singing a popular song in Venetian dialect: *Drio del Squero a San Trovaso, dove un giorno t'ho dà un baso* (Behind the Squero where once I kissed you...), though I cannot guarantee

And opposite it, an early evening throng outside Al Squero.

it. It is certainly a beckoning little world. The boathouse itself is a timber structure that looks as though it has been lifted straight out of the Tyrol, though its true origins lie in Cadore, a northern region of the Veneto famous for its foresters and woodworkers who migrated both seasonally and permanently to the Republic to work in the boatyards and shipyards. Cadore was also, incidentally, the birthplace of Titian: the mountain backdrops in many of his paintings are the work of an artist to whom such landscapes were familiar.

Sign at the junction of two canals alerting motor boats to gondola traffic.

I have chosen to juxtapose Soave with the gondola for the reason that both seem to suffer from the same preconceptions, easily dispelled on proper acquaintance. The gondola is often the victim of snobbery. Gondola rides are dismissed as a 'tourist rip-off'; wanting a ride in a gondola is, in some ill-defined sense, a badge of vulgarity. At the most basic level, it is hard to see how 80 or 90 euros, the price of a fairly indifferent meal for two in a great many restaurants here—or anywhere else for that matter—can be considered a rip-off for such an absorbing experience. At a higher level, the gondola is woven so intricately into both the historical and contemporary fabric of Venetian life that surely it is a mistake to disparage it. This not only was the craft that bore generations of Venetians of all types and social classes about their daily business. It also carried Byron, Hemingway and Browning along the Grand Canal and beyond, ferried Reynaldo Hahn and Nellie Melba along moonlit canals as they gave impromptu concerts, plied Stravinsky and Diaghilev to their final resting places on San Michele. And leaving aside these social and cultural associations, the gondola is also a masterpiece of nautical engineering and craftsmanship. No fewer than eight types of wood are used in the build: the finished craft is a gleaming compendium of lime, oak, mahogany, walnut, cherry, fir, larch and elm, each chosen for its specific adaptation to ornament, construction or navigability. And then there is the sophisticated asymmetrical design, developed over centuries and brought to final perfection over the last hundred years in the *squero* of Tramontin (also in Dorsoduro, on the Rio dell'Avogaria). The masterly computations of balance and compensation that have gone into the design over time makes the gondola, as the historian Horatio Brown aptly observed, an 'obedient' craft, reminding us that it is as fit for basic purpose as it is for ostentation, ceremony or romance. Brown died in Dorsoduro in 1926. His *Life on the Lagoons* is dedicated to his gondolier.

In the northern *sestiere* of Cannaregio there is a canal named Rio dei Lustraferri. I will admit that it has occurred to me that if ever a time should come when the going gets really rough, I might advertise myself as a *lustraferro*, literally an 'iron polisher', a person whose sole occupation is to polish the *ferro*, the scimitar-like, six-barbed crest that adorns the prow of the gondola. The six barbs are said to represent the six *sestieri* of Venice, while the barb that points backwards stands for the Giudecca. On more ornate *ferri*, you will see three smaller prongs interspersed between the main six, proclaiming Torcello, Murano and Burano. The uppermost curve of the blade recalls the Doge's ceremonial cap; the internal curve unmistakably celebrates the curling serpent that is the Grand Canal. If some eccentric millionaire with a gondola in his drawing-room were to advertise for such a post, I would have happily sat polishing his *ferro*, regaling his other staff with tales of life, love and loss on the Molo. What yarns I might spin for them! All Venetophiles will have their own favourite gondola vignettes. Mine are the following.

The first story illustrates the Sargasso Sea of laziness into which one's life can so easily slide here. It is a tale told against himself by the (largely forgotten) English watercolourist William Callow. One evening, towards sunset, having finished work for the day, Callow had taken a gondola out into the *Bacino*. There he lolled contentedly on the waters with a glass of wine, in a haze of cigar smoke and *dolce far niente*. Presently he noticed another gondola rocking

A gondola and its gleaming *ferro*. The six forward-facing prongs are said to stand for the six *sestieri* of Venice: San Marco, San Polo, Santa Croce, Cannaregio, Castello and Dorsoduro. Between them are three decorative finials representing the islands of Murano, Burano and Torcello. The backward-facing prong represents the Giudecca.

gently nearby, containing another young man, drinkless and cigarless, absorbed in sketching San Giorgio Maggiore in the light of the setting sun. It was a fellow artist, a man whose name lives on: J.M.W. Turner. 'I felt quite ashamed of myself,' wrote Callow, 'idling away my time whilst he was hard at work so late.'

The second vignette illustrates a gondola being put to a unique and possibly unprecedented use. 'In April 1894, a middle-aged gentleman, bearing a load of dresses, was rowed to the deepest part of the Venetian lagoon. A strange scene followed: he began to drown the dresses, one by one. There were a good many, well-made, tasteful, and all dark, suggesting a lady of quiet habits and some reserve. The gondolier's pole would have been useful for pushing them under the still water. But the dresses refused to drown.

9. OSTERIA AL SQUERO

One by one they rose to the surface, their busts and sleeves swelling like black balloons. Purposefully, the gentleman pushed them under, but silent, reproachful, they rose before his eyes.' The 'middle-aged gentleman' was Henry James, described here by his biographer, Lyndall Gordon. The supposed 'lady of quiet habits' was James's close friend, the American writer Constance Fenimore Woolson, who died having fallen from the window of her lodgings in Dorsoduro. The relationship between James and Fenimore Woolson remains an open question, but it is generally thought that she was in love with him, a fixation he was unable to requite. James's view was that she had committed suicide having lost her mind. Whatever the truth, the elaborate ceremony points, if not to a sense of guilt, then to an unsettling intensity of feeling on James's part. It went far beyond what might have been expected of him as he helped wind up her estate, a responsibility for which he had volunteered rather than been appointed.

In the 15th century there were some 10,000 gondolas on the water. In the 19th century, well-to-do Venetians would keep a gondolier much as other people kept a chauffeur. The last private gondola in Venice belonged to Peggy Guggenheim, who died in 1949. Today, the species has dwindled to 400. It is not endangered yet, but still, let us nurture and enjoy these creatures while we still can.

Al Todaro, a popular pit stop for thirsty gondoliers.

10. AL TODARO

Al Todaro is a small bar commanding a strategic position on the Piazzetta, at the southern corner of the Marciana Library (a superb example of Venetian Renaissance architecture, designed by Jacopo Sansovino and completed in 1588). The bar is hard by St. Theodore's column, hence its name, Todaro being the affectionate local moniker for Theodore, who was the city's patron saint until the ninth century, superseded when Mark's remains were triumphantly brought here from Alexandria. The arrival of the Evangelist inevitably put Theodore in the shade, but his cult lives quietly on, embodied in the theatrical statue that tops the column, showing him slaying a decidedly crocodilian dragon of Evil.

The tables nearest the column give views in all directions. To the north one sees the Torre dell'Orologio clock-tower; to the east St Mark's Basilica and the Doge's Palace; to the south the island of San Giorgio Maggiore; to the west the promenade leading to the Sailing Club and Harry's Bar, with the Giardini Ex Reali on the way. Al Todaro is famous above all for its ice creams, but when I sit here, as I often do, I usually order a Crodino, a sort of nursery-room drink, one of the non-alcoholic bitters manufactured under the Campari umbrella (Gingerino is another but I prefer Crodino). It was invented in 1965 and makes the usual sort of fuss about the secrecy of its recipe. I have no idea what herbs or chemicals go into it. It tastes pleasant and refreshing and it is customary to serve it on ice with a slice of orange and a green olive.

Al Todaro today is a popular place, and not only with tourists. Gondoliers pop in for a swift glug of something cool and refreshing before heading out to do another scull around the canals, and there are often decorous gatherings of elegant, elderly Venetian ladies enjoying the afternoon sunshine. I raise my glass to Al Todaro's founder, Giovanni Barsalich, a Paduan entrepreneur who started selling ice cream in Venice and the Veneto after the Second World War, operating out of a warehouse near Treviso that had previously served as an infirmary for Allied soldiers. Al Todaro was founded in 1948, an important year in Venice's post-war self-reconstruction. There is an interesting vestige of graffiti on one of the columns outside it, proclaiming the patriotic battle cry of the Republic: '*Viva San Marco, Viva la Repubblica!*' Uttering this slogan was made a capital offence during the Napoleonic occupation and Al Todaro is a good place to contemplate Napoleon, for here one sees so much evidence of the swift and ferocious dismantling of Venetian civic pride and identity that followed his conquest of Venice in 1797.

Patriotic graffito at Al Todaro:
Viva San Marco, Viva La Repubblica!

Having secured the city, Napoleon introduced draconian measures designed to obliterate as much as he could of its patriotic symbology. He defaced or destroyed scores of images of the Lion of St Mark. From the façade of St Mark's Basilica, he removed and sent to Paris the ancient Horses of St Mark's, brought to Venice from Constantinople in 1204 (their return was thanks to the diplomacy of the sculptor Canova; *see p. 51*); In the Piazza behind, he tore down the beautiful and ancient church of San Geminiano to make way for a ballroom, in the building that is now the Museo Correr. On the waterfront he destroyed the 14th-century Terranova granaries to create a formal 'royal' garden, the Giardini Reali. If one looks out across the water, one sees the island of San Giorgio Maggiore, which was the scene of a war crime of sorts, even though it involved the wilful destruction of an object as opposed to a person or a community. But it was perhaps Napoleon's most eloquent act of vandalism. In 1798 he ordered his soldiers to seize and destroy the *Bucintoro*, the state barge of the Doges of Venice.

Dating from 1727, this *Bucintoro* was the fifth and last incarnation of the state barge. A model of it can be seen in the Museo Navale near the Arsenale. Goethe saw it in 1786. 'The ship is overladen with ornament,' he tells us, 'completely covered in gilt carving. It has but one purpose: to be a monstrance, to exhibit to the people their leaders in splendid style. This state galley is a good indicator of

Coffee and a Crodino, impeccably served at Al Todaro.

who the Venetians were and how they saw themselves.' A monstrance, in the Catholic church, is an elaborate portable placard used for displaying the Communion bread to the congregation. It is the context in which a sacred symbol is displayed. Goethe believed that for the Venetians, the *Bucintoro* was just such a thing. And Napoleon set fire to it on the island San Giorgio, where it burned for four days. His troops salvaged as much molten gold and valuable fittings as they could, transporting the plunder into awaiting boats with the help of over 400 pack mules. Only the hull alone remained intact and was recycled as a coastal defence vessel.

The *Bucintoro* ended its miserable retirement as a squalid prison hulk before being dismantled and destroyed for good in 1824. A pile of rotting timber was all that remained.

The *Bucintoro* may have gone but there is another icon which, for me, illustrates equally well what the Venetians were and how they saw themselves. Now—perhaps fittingly— held by the Museo Correr, the museum of Venetian history in Napoleon's former ballroom wing, it is the prayer book of Doge Francesco Morosini (1619–94), who led Venice as Captain-General at the height of the Great Turkish War, before his election as Doge in 1688. We are told that he 'dressed always in crimson from head to toe, and never went forth without his cat beside him', even into battle. As well as Nini (this was the cat's name, although some say she was also called Dogaressa, a title normally reserved for doges' wives; Morosini never married) he always took care to carry with him his prayer book, a dummy prayer book in fact, with hollowed-out pages concealing a pistol that could be fired without opening the cover, by means of a silk drawstring attached to the trigger. As well as being as perfect an emblem of the uneasy relationship between Church and State as one is likely to find, the object also speaks eloquently of the perpetual precariousness that attended the fanfare and ostentation of the Republic and its autocrats, the sense of nagging paranoia and mistrust among the ruling patrician class and the climate of fear that held the fabric of state together for so long.

10. AL TODARO

Morosini remains a hero for the Venetians. The prestigious Naval Academy here is named after him and his gigantic sepulchral seal fills the floor at the west end of the church of Santo Stefano. He is seen as the last in a long line of warrior-doges, dauntlessly vigorous ruffians who held the Republic together until the decadence of its dying days. He had detractors too, notably Byron, who described him as 'the blundering Venetian, who blew up the Acropolis of Athens with a bomb'. Byron was referring to a decisive moment in the Turkish campaign when, in September 1687, Morosini bombarded the Ottoman powder magazine in the Parthenon, killing around 300 people and destroying the hitherto miraculously intact roof of the temple. Early the following year, an Elgin *avant la lettre*, he attempted to remove various sculptures from the Parthenon, notably the chariots and horses of Athena and Poseidon, which fell to the ground and smashed. Morosini contented himself with the Piraeus Lion, since before Christ the guardian of Piraeus harbour and a suitable spoil of war given its obvious symbolic association with St Mark. It still sits outside the Porta di Terra, the main land entrance to the Arsenale, and all campaigns for its restitution to Greece have so far been unsuccessful.

Morosini died as he had lived, on yet another turbulent expedition in the Peloponnese. Some years earlier, when Nini died, he had her embalmed and she too is now on display in the Correr. Morosini had her arranged harrying a gigantic stuffed rat, an appropriate symbol of the relentless ferocity with which he himself harried the enemies of the Republic.

Putting aside reflections on the antics of Napoleon and Morosini, before leaving Al Todaro, one might remember that this was also a favourite haunt of a gentler soul, Pope John XXIII, who used to take morning coffee here when he was Patriarch of Venice. Indeed, the small square on the other side of St Mark's is named after him: Piazzetta Papa Giovanni XXIII. His final encyclical, *Pacem in Terris* ('Peace on Earth', April 1963), dwelt on the relations between states and the rights and obligations of individuals. The messages it contains seems very far indeed from the days of the Ottoman-Venetian power struggle or the Napoleonic Wars: 'No country has the right to take any action that would constitute an unjust oppression of other countries, or an unwarranted interference in their affairs. No state can fittingly pursue its own interests in isolation from the rest nor, under such circumstances, can it develop itself as it should. The prosperity and progress of any state is in part consequence, and in part cause, of the prosperity and progress of all other states. No era will ever succeed in destroying the unity of the human family, for it consists of men who are all equal by virtue of their natural dignity.'

11. PALAZZETTO PISANI

The deconsecrated church of San Vidal stands at the Accademia Bridge end of Campo Santo Stefano. Many will know it for its concerts centred on Vivaldi, which take place all year round, no fewer than 360 nights a year. How does the orchestra, the Interpreti Veneziani, manage to keep itself fresh, given such a punishing and repetitive programme? The musical director once told me that he achieved this by regularly introducing additional material into the core repertoire. Thus *The Four Seasons* might be accompanied by a curiosity such as the concerto for double bass by Dittersdorf (a friend of Haydn) or an extravaganza by that magnificent amateur composer and violinist, Prince Johann Ernst of Saxe-Weimar (who had taken lessons from a cousin of Bach).

There are two hornet's nests one can stir up apropos Vivaldi: first, that his music is too 'popular'; second, that this very popularity is due in large measure to Ezra Pound, a vocal Fascist sympathiser.

San Vidal is very close to the Conservatorio Benedetto Marcello, Venice's distinguished music academy. I have always had a great affection for the Conservatorio; the pleasing sounds of tuning up and rehearsal echo daily across Campo Santo Stefano. On a fine summer morning many years ago, I remember marching in there, with no prior letter of introduction or permit, to try out a few of Bach's keyboard transcriptions of Vivaldi's concerti in one of the piano practice rooms. But a ferocious middle-aged woman burst in on me, very nearly as tiny and every bit as frightening as the axe lady in *Don't Look Now*. She said the practice rooms were out of bounds to the public and that I should leave immediately. Of course, I did—and all attempts to play myself into the mind of Ezra Pound ceased. Pound had loved the Bach-Vivaldi transcriptions and he played an important role in the Vivaldi revival that took place in the 1930s.

The Vivaldi revival was part of a sweeping cultural strategy put in place by Mussolini and his advisers, whereby the best aspects of Italian culture, from ancient Rome onwards, were co-opted as emblems of the regime. Ezra Pound and his mistress, the violinist Olga Rudge, were notable figures in this politicised reinvention of Vivaldi, whose work had been unfashionable in, if not entirely absent from, the mainstream concert repertoire since the 18th century. Rudge had unearthed a corpus of Vivaldi concerti in private collections in Turin, while Pound had discovered a similarly valuable hoard in the state collection in Dresden and had arranged

San Vidal: high altarpiece by Vittore Carpaccio.

to have microfilm copies made. Pound set about editing and transcribing it for publication and in 1936 assembled a local orchestra at Rapallo, on the Italian Riviera, to deliver a series of concerts devoted to the performance of the 'lost' works.

Antonio Vivaldi's music has been part of the popular repertoire ever since. Pound's reputation, however, remains mired in the poet's own anti-semitism. He voluntarily cast himself as 'Mussolini's megaphone'. He was stingingly condemned by George Orwell, in the *Partisan Review* in 1949: 'Pound was an ardent follower of Mussolini [...] and never concealed it. His broadcasts were disgusting [...] The opinions that he has tried to disseminate by means of his works are evil.' Ernest Hemingway, on the other hand, was one of his champions, praising the great beauty that intermittently shines from passages in the Cantos. Either view could be persuasive, depending on one's literary taste or talent for forgiveness. Pound's detractors have focused on his lack of remorse. His regret, confided late in life to Allen Ginsberg, that he had adopted what he called the 'suburban prejudice' of anti-Semitism, seems more a regret at appearing suburban than at being remembered as an anti-Semite. However, *quos deus vult perdere, prius dementat*: Pound was punished for his views, after the war. Having been arrested for treason and incarcerated in an open-air cage at a prison camp near Pisa, he lost his mind and subsequently languished in an asylum near Washington, DC. In the last years of his life he settled in Venice, where he lived for many years in Calle Querini in Dorsoduro. He and Olga are buried in the Protestant section of the cemetery at San Michele.

But when contemplating Vivaldi, what does one drink, and where? Vivaldi was a man of apparently distinctive appearance. When he took holy orders in 1703, he was swiftly nicknamed The Red Priest, on account of his shock of long red hair. There is an amusing caricature of him made in 1723, showing him in profile, with a large and beaky nose and an appealingly mischievous expression. The drawing is in monochrome ink, but knowing what one knows, it takes but a moment mentally to colour it in and bring it further to life. These physical attributes, in contrast to his sober calling and garb as a cleric, combined to make him a striking and memorable figure—and as a performer he was a formidable violinist. The German architect and musician Johann Friedrich Armand von Uffenbach heard him play: 'Vivaldi played a solo accompaniment excellently, and at the conclusion he added a free fantasy which absolutely astounded me, for it is hardly possible that anyone has ever played, or ever will play, in such a fashion.' As a teacher he was popular and effective, in his role as master of music at the Pio Ospedale della Pietà on the Riva Degli Schiavoni, a charitable foundation for orphans and children from poor families, where the boys would leave at fifteen with a trade under their belts while the girls were given a musical education as singers and instrumentalists. The French critic Charles de Brosses was one of many contemporary visitors who praised the concerts they regularly gave: 'One hears exceptional music at the Ospedale, where the *putte* [the girls] sing like angels and play the violin, the organ, the oboe, the cello and the bassoon; in short, there seems to be no instrument that intimidates them!' There is evidence of Vivaldi's personal engagement with his pupils. We learn from his notes that his very first composition for the Pietà, a C-major sonata for oboe, violin and organ (RV 779), was written for 'Pelegrina the oboist, Prudenza the contralto, Candida the viol player and Lucietta the organist'. From then on Vivaldi would routinely cite his star performers in this way. Vivaldi's music deserves its fame. Condemning him as 'too popular' is surely no more than would-be-sophisticated philistinism?

To celebrate him as I think he deserves, I have invented a cocktail: the *Prete Rosso* or 'Red Priest'. To find a person to mix it, I went to Palazzetto Pisani, a boutique hotel hidden away in a side street behind the Conservatorio Benedetto Marcello. Its bar is one of the few watering holes in Venice that can genuinely be described as a 'hidden treasure', so it is in a spirit of heavy-hearted but selfless reluctance that I now draw it to the reader's attention. Having walked through the dusky Sotoportego Pisani and found the little *calle* leading to the Grand Canal, one gains the discreet entrance of the hotel and climbs its candlelit staircase to the second floor and the bar, a beautiful high-ceilinged room with two balconies that afford a stupendous view across the Grand Canal, the panorama taking in the Salute and the Punta Della Dogana to one's left and the Accademia Bridge to one's right. The bar manager, Maestro Carlo, has become a good friend over the years. The Red Priest he mixes for me is excellent: it also seems an appropriate choice to toast not only Vivaldi but also two formidable rich Americans who at different times made Venice their home and left a lasting imprint on the city. The first is Winnaretta Singer, princesse de Polignac (1865–1943), a notable musical patron, whose protégés and friends included Fauré, Stravinsky, Poulenc, Diaghilev and De Falla. The second is Peggy Guggenheim (1898–1979), the art dealer and collector whose palace on the Grand Canal is now a world-famous museum housing works by Mondrian, Picasso, de Chirico, Braque, Miró and Dalí, as well as by her second husband, Max Ernst. Both women were heiresses: Singer to the fortune made by her father Isaac, the sewing-machine pioneer; Guggenheim to her grandfather Meyer's empire, built principally on mining and smelting. As you look out over the Canal from the Palazzetto Pisani balcony, the Guggenheim Foundation is to your far left, the Palazzo Contarini Polignac to your far right. Singer bought her palace in 1900, for her husband, prince Edmond de Polignac. Guggenheim bought hers in 1949, following her divorce from Max Ernst and her subsequent

The waterfront façade of Palazzo Venier dei Leoni, now home to the Peggy Guggenheim Collection.

decision to close her New York gallery and to make a new life in Europe. Though the two women lived decades apart and never met, there is a pleasing connection between them, bridging the gulf of time separating their sojourns in Venice. As one looks at the cared-for terrace of the Guggenheim museum today, it is difficult to imagine the derelict palace it once was, with weeds and moss growing on the now splendid waterfront. In the early 1900s, captivated by its ornamental decay, Winnaretta and her friend Isabelle de la Baume Pluvinel, who bought and restored Ca' Dario, used to

The bar-dining room of Palazzetto Pisani, its windows giving onto the Grand Canal.

hold impromptu picnic suppers there, attended by footmen and often in the company of Proust and his sometime lover, the composer Reynaldo Hahn.

Singer and Guggenheim are otherwise difficult to link together. They had little in common, unless one counts their robust commitment to amorous adventure. In Peggy's case, this meant the pursuit of men; in Winnaretta's it was women (Virginia Woolf famously remarked that given her outward appearance of respectability, one would hardly have suspected she had 'ravished half the virgins in Paris').

Music was not something that bound them. A former private secretary of Guggenheim's once told me—less than chivalrously—when I asked about her musical tastes, 'My dear boy, Peggy's idea of a musical *soirée* was to put *Le quattro stagioni* on the gramophone and sh*g the house gondolier.'

But that at least brings us back to Vivaldi. Peggy, it turns out, was a woman of musical discernment and her private secretary, in assuming otherwise, was falling into the classic trap. After one of Maestro Carlo's Prete Rosso cocktails, you will be fit to remind anyone who dares to be sniffy about *The Four Seasons* that J.S. Bach was a fan and to tell them that Rousseau liked it well enough to write a version for unaccompanied flute.

THE RED PRIEST
or
PRETE ROSSO

Ingredients: 1 part vodka, 1 part Select, 1 part red vermouth.

Method: Add the ingredients to the glass one by one. Stir well. Add ice and a twist of orange or lemon.

---

12. CHIOSCHETTO

Chioschetto, 'the little kiosk', is an agreeable shack of a bar halfway between the vaporetto stops of Zattere and San Biagio. It seems appropriate to drink beer here, in deference to what used to be a thriving brewery just over a century ago, across the water on the Giudecca. The old brewery building, built by the German architect Ernst Wullekopf, is now an exhibition space but in its heyday it bore the name Distilleria Veneziana, and later, Birra Pedavena-Dreher. Anton Dreher, a brewer from Vienna, had invented what we know today as lager in 1841. It was a fresh, crisp ale, pale blonde in colour, and fermented at a constant low temperature in a cool warehouse or *Lager*. When he expanded into Hungary, he found that the underground vaults of a disused limestone mine in southeast Budapest were perfect for his purpose. Before the age of refrigeration, lager required either conditions such as these, or ready access to ice, which meant that in Italy, the only places realistically suitable for brewing were the alpine regions. The Luciani brothers, from Pedavena in the Venetian Dolomites, acquired the Italian arm of the Dreher business

12. CHIOSCHETTO

Chioschetto on the Zattere, looking over the Giudecca Canal.

in 1928. They did not use the Giudecca site for brewing; instead the Dreher building became a sales and distribution centre. Pedavena was largely acquired by Heineken in the 1970s. Brewing in the Venetian Dolomites today is now in the hands of Birra Castello, whose beers are available at Al Chioschetto.

The view from here, across the Giudecca Canal, is particularly fine. Dominating it, near the old Dreher building, is the huge neo-Gothic Molino Stucky, also built by Wullekopf. It is now a hotel, the Venice Hilton, but

Molino Stucky and the Fortuny factory on the Giudecca.

over a century ago it was a thriving flour mill, owned by the Swiss Stucky dynasty, once the richest family in Venice. In the distance, to the right, one sees the Blakeian 'Satanic Mills' of Marghera on the mainland, with their towering chimneys soaring above the distinctive rainbow-arc of the petrochemical pipeline bridge. Next to Molino Stucky is the plain, three-storey Fortuny factory and fabric showroom, with FORTUNY in large, angular, Art Deco capitals. You can admire plenty of fabrics there. But to see original examples of Fortuny's work, you need to visit the master designer's former home.

12. AL CHIOSCHETTO

Once a thriving studio and workshop-factory, Palazzo Pesaro degli Orfei on Campo San Benedetto in the *sestiere* of San Marco, is now open as the Museo Fortuny. Mariano Fortuny y Madrazo (1871–1949), the son of a Catalan artist, was at once painter, lighting engineer, inventor, textile manufacturer, fashion designer and Venice's Spanish Consul. In 1889 he settled in the city and in 1898 moved into Palazzo Pesaro, originally occupying the attic, though gradually acquiring more and more space until, by 1907, nearly the entire *palazzo* was given over to his workforce,

'What sets a Fortuny fabric apart is the way light seems to be inherent in the weave'.

over 100 strong, busily realising his fabric designs under the exacting personal supervision of Fortuny himself and his energetic wife, muse and general manager, Henriette Nigrin. After Fortuny's death in 1949, the building was donated to the city on condition that it be used in perpetuity as a cultural centre related to the arts. When Nigrin died in 1965, the Comune took full possession. Today, after a superb refit and restoration, the museum remains what it always has been, one of the most captivating interiors in Venice. The museum is so cleverly arranged to suggest a home that one feels like a trespasser, a too-early guest perhaps, nervously awaiting the arrival of Mariano and Henriette. Fortuny's self-portrait is on display, as well as his likeness of Henriette, whom he painted wearing the fabulous Delphos dress she designed and which can still be bought in the Fortuny boutique in San Marco.

If one were to set oneself the task of summing up Fortuny's work in one word, then 'light' would probably be the most appropriate choice. His ceiling lamps, whose patterned fabric shades cast a warm, diffused glow, hang in the saloons of his *palazzo* and on the second *piano nobile* one can see a large and superb model of his set and lighting design for the fourth act of *Das Rheingold* at Bayreuth. Fortuny was a master of light, but also of colour and texture. What sets a Fortuny fabric apart is the way light seems to be inherent in the weave. No doubt this is merely the result of his illusionistic technique, using complex layers of screen-printing to confer a painterly

Museo Fortuny.

A table at Chioschetto, with a bottle of Castello beer and a distant view of San Giorgio Maggiore, waiting for golden hour when the buildings will be bathed in a Henry Jamesean pink glow.

third dimension on what might otherwise have been a two-dimensional surface. Nonetheless, there does seem to be a supernatural quality in a Fortuny textile, if by an act of faith one might believe that light has been captured in the fabric, giving a soul to the body.

'Venice!' gasps Proust in *Albertine Disparue*, 'I had dreamed of it incessantly...the Fortuny gown which Albertine was wearing that evening seemed to me the tempting phantom of that invisible Venice. It swarmed with Arabic ornaments, like the Venetian palaces hidden like sultanas behind a screen of pierced stone, like the bindings in the Ambrosian library, like the columns from which the Oriental birds that symbolised alternatively life and death were repeated in the mirror of the fabric, of an intense blue which, as my gaze extended over it, was changed into a malleable gold...and the sleeves were lined with a cherry pink which is so peculiarly Venetian that it is called Tiepolo pink.' (Tr. C.K. Scott-Moncrieff)

Proust was not the only writer to notice the peculiarity of the Venetian pink. 'Asked what may be the leading colour in the Venetian concert,' mused Henry James (as if a concert *had* a colour), 'we should inveterately say Pink.' He was looking across the Giudecca Canal when this thought occurred to him, looking out at the same view as I am, when I sit at Al Chioschetto. It faces west, which makes it a perfect vantage point from which to watch the sunset, sipping a cool beer, admiring the 'concert' of colours in the lagoon water and sky.

13. BA'GHETTO

Ba'Ghetto is a kosher bar-restaurant in the Campo del Ghetto Nuovo in Cannaregio. You can enter its secluded courtyard garden from the *campo*, or arrive by taxi at the water-gate on Rio della Misericordia. In late spring and throughout summer and autumn, the garden is an enchanting place for an early evening drink and what tempts me when I come here is a lightly chilled, sparkling dessert wine, Bartenura Moscato d'Asti. Bartenura wines take their name from a 15th-century rabbi, Obadiah ben Abraham, who lived in Bertinoro ('Bartenura') in Emilia-Romagna, west of Rimini. The Moscato d'Asti is best served cool and drunk young. My invariable ritual, at Ba'Ghetto, is to raise a glass of it to Michelangelo Guggenheim (1837–1914), a prominent and glamorous figure in 19th-century Venice and one of the most successful and flamboyant art and antique dealers of his day.

The answer to the first question most people ask when his name is mentioned is 'No': there is no evidence to suggest any family connection with Peggy Guggenheim. Peggy's grandfather, Meyer Guggenheim, emigrated to the

USA from Lengnau in Switzerland in 1847. Michelangelo's parents, Samuel and Sara, emigrated to Venice from Baden-Württemberg in southern Germany in the mid-1820s. Both families belonged to successive waves of Jewish migration in the long-lasting wake of the Napoleonic Wars. While the great majority opted for the American dream, as Meyer did, there were those like Samuel and Sara who chose destinations closer to home. The existence of a long-established Jewish community in Venice might have played a part in Samuel's decision. His love of art, too, seems to have been a decisive factor—and naming his son Michelangelo proved an apt if unusual choice.

There is an interesting record of Michelangelo's rags-to-riches story in the diaries of his lifelong client and friend, Enid Layard. Enid's husband, Sir Austen Henry Layard, a prominent archaeologist and collector, had retired to Venice in 1878, though the Layards had been regular visitors for years, having bought the Ca' Capello, a *palazzo* on the Grand Canal, in 1869. The Venetian entries in Lady Layard's diaries from 1869 to 1905 give a clear—if socially circumscribed—picture of expatriate life in the city. We learn that the Layards had first met Guggenheim long before his spectacular success as a dealer: 'His father was one of the humblest of Jews & had a small shop near the Canonica [the clergy house adjoining St Mark's Basilica] where Henry used to go in early days in search of old things. Henry used to employ

Ba'Ghetto.

the son to go on errands & buy old things for him for a small remuneration.' Despite the fortune that later came to young Michelangelo, Lady Layard is pleased to note that he never forgot his early connection to her husband.

Guggenheim rapidly built up a thriving business and amassed an important private collection of art and antiques. He was renowned not only as a dealer but as a furniture designer, interior decorator, scholar, collector and energetic participant in the cultural and economic life of Venice. He lived in grand style in Palazzo Balbi, on the Grand Canal, which he had restored himself and where he met and entertained a distinguished circle of friends and clients. One of his most elaborate projects was the renovation of the interior of Palazzo Papadopoli, undertaken for the wealthy Corfiot family who owned it. The results were too flashy for Lady Layard: 'We went to the Papadopoli ball which is a few doors from us. The room looked splendid & the house has just been entirely done up by Guggenheim for 90,000 Fcs but it looks rather too much like a shopman's taste.' There were snobbish barbs directed at Guggenheim in the international press too, a good example being from an 1898 article in the *American Architect and Building News*: 'A lapse of social prestige similar to that of the Palazzo Foscari attaches to the Palazzo Balbi, designed by Alessandro Vittoria in the seventeenth century, and [...] from whose balconies leaned Napoleon and Josephine when they were still lovers. [It] is now the factory of a Mr Guggenheim, the vulgar display of whose name mars the façade...' As if lounging on a balcony with one's mistress were not an embodiment of vulgar display.

There is a charming *carte de visite* portrait of Guggenheim dating from around 1872, the year he met the Venetian art critic Giovanni Morelli. The 36-year-old dealer is handsome, good-humoured and seems manifestly confident, with a touch of dandified flamboyance. Morelli was instantly charmed and the two were to become friends and occasional collaborators in the sale and acquisition of important works of art. Morelli was particularly impressed by Guggenheim's prediction that the Americans would be the next great collectors, replacing the Grand Tour *cognoscenti*, who had been consistently faithful buyers up until the last quarter of the 18th century. Guggenheim was quick to cultivate Isabella Stewart Gardner, a leading light among the new American connoisseurs, to whom he sold a vast quantity of important objects, ranging from textiles and jewellery to the famous Black Glass Madonna, an early 17th-century Venetian devotional piece.

Michelangelo's first major coup as a picture dealer came in 1870, following the death of Count Giovanni Querini Stampalia, the Venetian entrepreneur and philanthropist who endowed the well-known foundation that bears his name. Paralysed by death duties, the newly formed Fondazione Querini Stampalia was forced to consider its

Tiepolo's *Triumph of Marius* from Ca' Dolfin, now in the Metropolitan Museum in New York.

position and decide which of its assets it should liquidate. A prime candidate was Ca' Dolfin, an ancient palace near San Pantalon in the *sestiere* of Dorsoduro. One of its principal rooms contained an important series of paintings by Tiepolo, depicting scenes from Roman martial history: *The Triumph of Marius*, *Cincinnatus Offered the Dictatorship*, *Veturia Pleading with Coriolanus*, and more. This 'Roman' room was awkwardly shaped and contained troublesome earlier design schemes, to the extent that Tiepolo was forced to take extra pains to ensure that his series fitted seamlessly and harmoniously into the available space. First Michelangelo bought the Tiepolo paintings for 6,000 lire, then the entire palace for a further 16,500. In a brisk flurry of asset-stripping, he removed the Tiepolos from the *salone* and sold them to one of his clients, the Austrian collector Baron Eugen von Miller zu Aichholz. Over the last century the series has been broken up and dispersed, and individual paintings can be seen as far afield as New York, Vienna and St Petersburg. Much has been written about the theoretical possibility of reuniting them and reinstating the entire scheme. Mirrors now fill the spaces left by those Roman scenes, ideal perhaps for taking a good long look at ourselves before we are too quick to condemn Michelangelo's picture deal.

In later life, as it turned out, Michelangelo himself came to deplore the very kind of behaviour he had once so eagerly embraced. As his fortune increased, he invested widely in the cultural heritage of the city: he donated generous tranches of his collection of Venetian textiles and artefacts to the Correr; he spoke and wrote passionately about the need for the sensitive and well-informed restoration of monuments; he took an energetic interest in promoting Venetian craftsmen— carpenters, carvers, gilders, glassblowers, lacemakers.

How this last task was achieved is interesting because it would be easy to make a case against Michelangelo as the founding father of dubious antiques reproduction. Every harpsichord that opens out into an illuminated drinks cabinet, every Louis Quinze shower-head and bidet set, every neo-Baroque personal gymnasium—all these belong to a lineage directly traceable back to the Guggenheim workshops in Venice. As his parallel career as a decorator went from strength to strength, Michelangelo rapidly realised that the available supply of important Renaissance and Baroque furniture and fittings was inadequate to fulfil the demand he had created. Based on extant drawings he therefore set about creating faithful and scholarly reproductions of original pieces. These were not passed off meretriciously as the real thing (Guggenheim was no forger); they were bought and sold as objects of value in their own right. A testimony to the meticulous research he undertook in the course of making replicas is the book he published in 1897, *Le Cornici Italiane* (*Italian Frames*), the first study to explore the history and design of frames in their own right, rather than as subsidiary ornamental components. Along the way, he would 'rescue' important early pieces from loss or decay, reserving them for his collection and making commercial copies of them for clients. All these enterprises conferred considerable benefit on the local community. We can easily forget that beneath the ornamental poverty we see in so many irritating paintings of the period, by John Humphreys Johnstone and others, there was large-scale unemployment in Venice and a crushing air of decay and dereliction. Michelangelo Guggenheim saw an opportunity and seized it, single-handedly reviving the glass, textile and woodworking mini-industries, consistently reinvesting his profits in new and, for the time, visionary ventures. His name lives on in Venice, but only in a largely overlooked corner of the city not generally accessible to the public. The cloisters of the Carmini in Dorsoduro are home to the Liceo Statale Michelangelo Guggenheim, an art school with a focus on artistic practice, architectural theory, graphic design and multimedia studies.

So—a glass of Bartenura Moscato d'Asti. Sparkling wine that comes in a bright blue bottle. Sweet and cloying? For vulgarians rather than the true connoisseur? Not a bit of it. It's marvellous stuff, the best expression of the Moscato Bianco grape, grown in the foothills of the Alps in the Italian region of Piedmont. It has been popular since Roman times: Coriolanus, Marius and Cincinnatus would all have come down from their painted ceiling for a glass of this.

14. HOTEL EXCELSIOR

The Blue Bar at the Grand Hotel Excelsior on the Venice Lido remains one of my favourite watering holes in Venice. I have many happy memories of it; there is always a sense of often unexpected theatricality to be enjoyed at the Excelsior. The mad, mock-Moorish riot of its dome and minarets against the azure sky always puts me in a good mood.

Bathing cabins on the Lido, in front of the Hotel Excelsior.

14. HOTEL EXCELSIOR

The Excelsior was completed and opened in 1908, designed by the architect Giovanni Sardi and commissioned by two important figures in the early 20th-century regeneration of Venice, Nicolò Spada and Count Giuseppe Volpi di Misurata. Spada was the founder of the Italian hotel group CIGA, while Volpi was an entrepreneur who progressively transformed the post-Austrian 19th-century city into a glamorous destination fit to compete with the French Riviera. Spada, as a hotelier, was keen to create an atmosphere that would subliminally remind travellers of the great European spas but offer something a little more liberated. First-time visitors might well be struck by Giovanni Sardi's extraordinarily eclectic Veneto-Byzantine-Moorish extravaganza, by its exuberant sense of space, by the sheer scale of the building inside and out, a grandeur as much in evidence in the suites as in the public spaces. This was Spada's intention, to create a sense of fantasy, luxury and freedom—and it worked, to the extent that by the 1920s the Excelsior, and the Venice Lido itself, had become an indispensable part of the upmarket tourist's annual pilgrimage.

Giuseppe Volpi's most significant contribution came much later, in 1932, when he made the inspired decision to hold an international exhibition of film in Venice as part of the already well-established Biennale. The Venice Biennale had been founded in 1885 and had gone from strength to strength as its 'national pavilions' were progressively built in the Giardini di Castello from 1907. Volpi made a shrewd assessment of the boom in the motion picture industry, following the advent of the 'talkies', and decided that a cinematic wing to the festival would draw in a fresh wave of visitors. As a minister in Mussolini's government and a powerful businessman in his own right, Volpi was able quietly to dispose of the various objections that were put forward. At the first 'Esposizione Internazionale d'Arte Cinematografica', which took place on the Excelsior terrace in 1932, Rouben Mamoulian's *Dr Jekyll and Mr Hyde* was the first film screened. During the war, perhaps inevitably, the Festival became a showcase for Italian and Nazi propaganda but in 1946 and 1947 it was relaunched in all its international splendour.

No visit to the Excelsior can really be complete without a drink at the Blue Bar. Its manager is Lino Marchese, a sophisticated mixologist and worthy successor to the great Tony Micelotta, who recently retired, loaded with honours both by the hospitality industry and the Italian government. Marchese is a great innovator and has created a new range of cocktails for the Blue Bar, many of them distinguished by a subtlety and lightness of touch that makes them beckoning alternatives to the old-school heavies like Dry Martini and Negroni. What I really look for in a new cocktail, though, is specificity, a focused sense of time and place. An example

of this is the Montgomery at Harry's Bar. Invented by Ernest Hemingway, it is a fifteen-to-one mix of gin and vermouth, the name a reference to the great Field Marshal's policy of preferably never launching an attack unless one outnumbers the enemy in this advantageous ratio. At the Blue Bar I think Marchese's great masterpiece of specificity is the Excelsior Ruby, where the intention has been to sum up in a single drink the glamour and aesthetic of both the Excelsior and the Lido. The result is enchanting, calling to mind not only one's own luxurious memories but also presenting an enticing picture of unbuttoned frolic yet to come. At the Venice Cocktail Week in 2021 the ingredients were given as Gin dei Sospiri (*see p. 124*); Select and Campari (more of the former than the latter; *for Select, see pp. 44–5*); fresh lime juice and elderberry syrup. The resulting ruby-red cocktail is served in a gold-rimmed goblet, a pleasing antiquarian

DEATH IN VENICE

Ingredients: Italian dry white vermouth to perfume the glass. 75ml vodka, Cîroc if possible. Strawberry aquavit to taste. A twist of fresh lemon.

Method: Stir the vodka and strawberry aquavit with ice and strain into a chilled cocktail glass sprayed with the vermouth. Garnish with the lemon twist.

touch. One closes one's eyes and thinks of Isadora Duncan dancing along the Lido beach at sunset.

The Lido beach is also famous for the role it plays in Thomas Mann's well-known novella *Death in Venice*. And, admirer of the Excelsior Ruby though I am, I still think that the Death in Venice cocktail, which I constructed here with Tony Micelotta, has yet to be beaten for specificity. Its base spirit is Cîroc vodka, an allusion to the scirocco wind that blows banefully through the novel. This is blended with strawberry aquavit, to remind one of Aschenbach's fatal dish of overripe summer fruit. It is garnished with lemon and drunk from a splayed coupe. The recipe is given opposite.

The Death in Venice cocktail.

15. TiME SOCIAL BAR

Time is the key word with this bar in Cannaregio. In a city that puts itself to bed notoriously early, it is reassuring to know there is somewhere that stays open into the small hours. Other late-night options in Venice are few and they require stamina. Bars in Campo Santa Margherita can stay open until 2 or 3am, but one has to be prepared to engage in, or tolerate, the hurly-burly of the square. Piccolo Mondo, the smallest and most delightfully dated nightclub in Europe, hard by the Accademia, though fun and well worth a visit, is noisy and crowded. The TiME Social Bar, by contrast, with its industrial-chic interior, retro policy as regards music and elaborate cocktail menu, is a haven. The drinks list is innovative and changed quite often, though there are popular favourites that have stood the test of time. A number of them make use of Gin dei Sospiri, a Venetian artisan gin made with Sant'Erasmo glasswort. Alessandro Beggio is the driving force behind TiME and his philosophy is based on a love of and respect for 'local and national ingredients'—and deadening though that marketing phrase may be, the result is something to be thankful for.

TiME Social Bar.

Despar Teatro Italia.

15. TiME SOCIAL BAR

The same philosophy informs the nearby supermarket, Despar Teatro Italia, housed in a restored former theatre and cinema designed and completed by Giovanni Sardi in 1913. When it first opened as a supermarket, there was controversy about the 'sacrilege' of putting Giovanni Sardi's theatre building to such unashamedly commercial use. Venetophiles both local and international are resistant to change and hanker after an ornamental past—nearly as imaginary as it is economically untenable—populated by booksellers, butchers, bakers and candlestick makers on every street corner, all paying a peppercorn rent. The truth is that when the law regarding property use was relaxed in the seventies, landlords in Venice immediately cashed in, either with a flurry of hotels and apartments, or with high-rent ground-floor retail premises. This caused an exodus to the mainland of Venetians who could no longer afford to rent property in town, and an explosion of tourist-orientated retailers who, unlike traditional artisans, could afford the higher prices much more easily. Now, though, we are seeing some imaginative attempts to heal the scars caused by misdirected market forces and an important virtue of the new supermarket is that it affords an outlet for a wide variety of manufacturers and suppliers who could not afford to rent retail premises of their own—an elegant solution that might easily be adapted to the needs of butchers, bakers and candlestick makers in many other large and disused buildings in the city.

A mural of Michelangelo's *David* from the old Teatro Italia helps one ponder the selection of bread rolls.

Putting all this to one side, though, one should allow oneself time to admire the restrained eclecticism of Sardi's building and the various decorations supplied by his collaborators. The façade is adorned with a central, neo-Gothic, triple lancet window with tracery recalling the Doge's Palace and Palazzo Foscari. This is flanked by a pair of pleasingly restrained single-lancet windows and the façade is crowned by an elegant balustrade with a central relief of the Lion of St Mark. The wrought-iron entrance gates were designed by Umberto Bellotto, a Venetian metalworker and glassmaker who also made the chandeliers inside. The ceiling of the main hall is decorated with an allegorical painting, *The Glory of Italy*, by Alessandro Pomi. The Art Nouveau decorations throughout the hall were completed by the Friulan artist Guido Marussig and various other local artists. Though one would never guess it on first inspection, the building was one of the first in Venice to rely on reinforced concrete in its construction. It is a perfect example of its genre and period and as such leads one to reflect on the many examples of good and bad pastiche one encounters in the city.

There have been two distinct strains of pastiche architecture in Venice. At one end of the spectrum you have Edoardo Trigomi Mattei's Palazzo Genovese (1892), built next to the Salute on a site created by razing what remained of the old abbey cloisters and gardens of San Gregorio. It

Artisanal cocktail at TiME Social.

now houses the Centurion Palace Hotel. The bar is excellent, overlooking the Grand Canal, but the building itself is an example of neo-Gothic at its deadest and most wooden. Further up the Grand Canal is Palazzetto Stern (now also a hotel and also with an excellent bar), completed by Carlo Mainella in 1911 for the would-be society hostess Ernesta de Hierschel Stern. It is a twee fairycake of a building, its patchy and meanly fenestrated façade a decorative mockery of the stately spirit of the old Venetian Gothic. Of course, there is a strong argument for saying that poor neo-Gothic is a less deleterious phenomenon than aggressive Modernism: there are far worse buildings than the Centurion and the Stern. But at the best end of the spectrum there are three architects whose work established some coherent link between the old and the new, as well as being dignified by original innovation. One is Domenico Rupalo, architect of the Rialto Fish Market, completed in 1911 and arguably— given the central role it continues to play in everyday life— the most important neo-Gothic building in Venice. A second is Giuseppe Torres, who built a superb Venetian-Byzantine-Gothic house for himself and his family on Fondamenta del Gaffaro in Dorsoduro. And the third is Giovanni Sardi. What unifies these three very different architects and sets them apart from copybook practitioners of Revival styles, is what Venetians have called *venezianismo*, the quality not only of replicating the form of bygone architecture but simultaneously of channelling its spirit, adding thoughtful contemporary flourishes that harmonise with the fabric of the city and suit the contemporary context. Thoughtful eclecticism at its best, in other words. Giovanni Sardi not only built the Teatro Italia; he also designed the mad Moorish extravaganza that is the Grand Hotel Excelsior on the Lido (*see p. 118*). Whenever I find myself in the TiME Social Bar, it is to him that I raise my cocktail glass.

16. GRITTI PALACE

The Gritti Palace is one of the most famous hotels in Venice, a 15th-century *palazzo* that has been attracting guests to its cosy opulence since 1895. And its Bar Longhi is a superb place to drink. Along with Harry's and Caffè Florian it belongs to that Holy Trinity of expensive Venice bars that are worth every last cent of the bill. The bar counter itself—a Baroque altar-surround from a Sicilian church—presides over several acres of plush, Rubelli fabric and three original paintings by Pietro Longhi, the painter after whom the bar is named and whose genre scenes provide a little window on 18th-century Venetian life. The designer responsible for this paradise (and for a complete makeover of the entire hotel) is Chuck Chewning, a man who, for his twelfth birthday, asked his parents for a subscription to *Architectural Digest*. The terrace of Bar Longhi has a nautical feel to it. With its cream leather seats and teak tabletops, it is Riva-branded, to make you feel as if you are on board a sleek water taxi—or even a superyacht or ocean liner. The terrace commands one of the best views in the city, across the Grand Canal to Santa Maria della Salute.

Setting up tables on the terrace of the Bar Longhi, Gritti Palace.

The church of the Salute.

The Salute's domed silhouette is, of course, an established Venetian icon, celebrated by great *vedutisti* such as Guardi and Canaletto and later by host of formidable expatriate artists led by Turner, Sargent and Monet.

'*Salute*' means 'health', in reference to the church having been built as an act of supplication following the Plague of 1630, in which some 46,000 people in central Venice perished (about a third of the population) and a further 96,000 around the lagoon. As the Plague intensified, it became clear that the customary round of prayer and procession was doing little to decelerate the death toll, so the Senate felt it appropriate to build and dedicate an elaborate church to Our Lady of Health—as much an exercise in rebuilding popular morale as it was a devout insurance policy against further catastrophe. A competition to design the building was won by the Venetian architect Baldassare Longhena (1598–1682), whose proposal brightly outshone those of his ten rivals, all of whom submitted rectilinear designs in the Palladian tradition. No doubt they sought to echo Palladio's Redentore, a supplicatory response to an earlier plague, but Longhena was determined to create a new Venetian horizon. As he put it, 'I have created a church in the form of a rotunda, a work of new invention, never built in Venice. This church [...] being dedicated to the Blessed Virgin made me think, with what little talent God has bestowed upon me, of building it in the shape of a crown.' The project was begun in 1631 and happily Longhena lived just long enough to see it completed fifty years later. It had taken half a century—two if not three generations in those days—a labour difficult to appreciate clearly through the distorted prism of our mushrooming, high-rise age. Even before the first slabs of the church itself could be put in place, two decades of work went into the foundations. Beneath the Salute and its waterfront platform, no fewer than a million wooden piles stand shoulder to shoulder in the seabed, bearing the weight of Longhena's splendid Baroque 'crown', silent and invisible witnesses to this curious and spectacular labour of love.

In our own century the Salute once again found itself fulfilling its role as Venice's principal Plague church. By mid-

May 2020, Italy had recorded 1,250 deaths from Covid-19. Considering with hindsight what was yet to come, this does not seem alarming but at the time Italy was bearing the brunt of the pandemic more than any other country in Europe. The Patriarch of Venice, Cardinal Francesco Moraglia, composed a special prayer which was read out by the Mayor of Venice, Luigi Brugnaro, during a service in the Salute. The quarantine measures that Venice took against disease over the centuries form a staple topic for all tour guides. Yet only a few years ago, those same measures, or something very like them, were adopted again. In the distant past, Venetians had resolutely embraced the draconian forty-day *quarantena*, set in place by the Republic amid the ravages of the Black Death in the 14th century. In 2020, they quietly but swiftly embraced them again, with an exemplary Venetian mix of resilience, frustration, humour and practicality.

Now that happier days have returned, at least for a while, the Bar Longhi is an excellent place to come to enjoy a cocktail and to toast the view of the Salute. The Bar Longhi offers a cocktail called the Doge Gritti, a variation on the Negroni theme named after Doge Andrea Gritti (1455–1538), whose home this was. The Doge Gritti cocktail is made of gin, vermouth and orange bitters. If this seems too festive a drink to honour the severe figure we see kneeling in stone before the Lion of St Mark on the façade of the Doge's Palace (above the central window facing the Piazzetta), then a brief meditation on Gritti's life and achievements is certainly in order.

On should really raise not one but three respectful bumpers to Andrea Gritti, libations for three very different but closely interrelated aspects of his life: merchant, soldier-politician, patron of the arts—a very Venetian combination. Gritti enjoyed a long and lucrative career as a grain dealer in Constantinople. Despite an interlude of imprisonment for espionage and a growing reputation for amatory adventures, he nonetheless left Constantinople in good standing with Sultan Bayezıt II, later enabling him to negotiate a welcome if short-lived peace treaty with the Turks following yet another

---

DOGE GRITTI

Ingredients (NB: The exact proportions required are known only to Bar Longhi mixologists): Gin, Carpano Antica Formula vermouth, Maraschino cherry liqueur, orange bitters.

Method: Tip a handful of ice cubes into a tumbler. Pour in the gin, then the vermouth, then the Maraschino. Drop in the bitters. Stir, garnish with orange.

---

outbreak of Venetian-Ottoman hostility. When he was fifty, Gritti embarked on a second career as politician, soldier and diplomat, adroitly reducing the impact on the Republic of wars in Italy and Europe, maintaining on Venice's behalf a cunning neutrality in the ongoing conflict between Charles V, the Holy Roman Emperor, and the French king Francis I. And finally, Gritti's patronage of the arts. He is memorable as much for his refined taste as for his calculating awareness of the value of coaxing leading artists into the service of the state. Unlike many autocrats, he was no indiscriminate gatherer of random and willing talent. When the great architect and sculptor Jacopo Sansovino found himself a refugee from Rome, following its the sack by Charles V in 1527, Gritti persuaded him to settle in Venice. Gritti was a champion of Titian, who painted some revealing and deeply personal portraits of him. My favourite, now in the National Gallery of Art in Washington, speaks of an unmistakable rapport between artist and sitter. Here I think one can clearly see the true spirit of the 77th Doge of Venice. Beneath the savagely beetling brows there is an engaging flicker of a smile. Under the heavy velvet robes of autocracy, each golden button as large as a bread roll, lurks a wry worldliness, a sadness even. As one surveys Titian's reading of his patron, it comes as no surprise to learn from contemporary accounts that Andrea Gritti was a cheerful companion at dinner. I think he would have enjoyed the cocktail that has been named in his honour.

Doge Andrea Gritti,
by Titian (1540s).

17. LA CALCINA

As a large plaque on the front elevation proudly proclaims, Hotel La Calcina on the Zattere was John Ruskin's home in Venice in the spring of 1877. Its restaurant-bar was also a meeting point for Italian luminaries, including Verdi's librettist Francesco Maria Piave and the singer and actress Ornella Vanoni, not to mention Professor Carlo Rubbia, winner of the 1984 Nobel Prize for Physics. Yet since it is easily argued that Ruskin has contributed more to the heritage of Venice than any of these, it seems only fair to raise a glass to him.

In season, the Calcina bar serves excellent oysters and when possible, I like to pair half a dozen of them with a Gin and Tonic. The thinking is partially gourmet-inspired, but the idea of gin and oysters has a suitably archaic and very English ring to it, harking back to a century and a half ago, when both were common staples affordable by the plain working man whom Ruskin sought so passionately to elevate. At all events, this is the perfect spot to ponder the life and work of this complex, passionate man, to engage with his prejudices and attempt to understand how this

The bar at La Calcina.

city touched his soul and tempered his being for over half a century. One of those prejudices—the architecture of Palladio—comes unavoidably to mind as one looks over the Giudecca Canal towards the Redentore. So I raise my glass in its direction.

It should be said that the team at La Calcina are admirable purists when it comes to Gin and Tonic. They always make sure that my glass is never over-laden with ice or garnished with anything more from the orchard or herb bed than a simple slice of lime or lemon. And I am left to add my own tonic, in whatever measure I choose. This is an important consideration in an age when simple drinks, that have stood the test of time and need no drastic makeovers, are frequently subjected to superfluous elaboration. Gin and Tonic is always available at La Calcina, but there are rumours that they are working on a new cocktail in honour of Ruskin—a development much to be applauded.

There is a palpable bitterness about Ruskin's 1877 sojourn at La Calcina, viewed against the triumphs, a quarter of a century earlier, of *The Stones of Venice* (1851–3). The intention was to revise and extend his earlier survey. All that resulted, however, was an incomplete cycle of paintings and a further text, *St Mark's Rest*, that is seldom read today, though it is an intriguingly personal account of Ruskin's engagement with Venice. He was losing his touch, or so he felt, as this melancholy passage from his diary attests: 'A marvellous sunset from St Elena, with returning storm over Treviso. But all passes now without leaving more than a trace in memory, and I can't note the tenth part of it for use. Thus, I've already forgotten the sunset of the 9th, and only on seeing the entry, call back the crimson on San Giorgio and the Salute and the ships' masts, all fire.' This recalls the endearing spirit of humility that shone forth from his early paintings, and the notes that he made on them, particularly

GIN AND TONIC

Ingredients: 50ml plain London gin, 1 small bottle unflavoured Indian tonic water. One slice of lemon or lime to garnish. That's it.

Method: Put a small number of ice cubes into a straight-sided tumbler or balloon. Add the slice of lemon or lime. Pour the gin over. Serve the tonic separately, to be added by the customer *ad lib*.

in letters to his father, where he deplores a lack of technical ability to reveal his full understanding of what he observes. In 1877 he has returned to this formative state, but without the broad vista of the future ahead of him.

A striking quality of those early paintings, ranging from misty alpine views to microscopic studies of leaves and carvings, is that they are not mere attempts at depiction. They seem as much to be investigative attempts to

Palladio's façade of San Giorgio Maggiore, with its interlocking play of pediments and other elements borrowed from Classical architecture.

understand the fabric, texture and construction of both natural and man-made objects. This is worth bearing in mind as one considers his later project, of revealing the form and substance of Venice to the broader reading public, when his efforts were not solely restricted to the meticulous and magnificent architectural survey one sees in *The Stones of Venice*. Ruskin also successfully took part-ownership of ongoing local attempts to restore and preserve the city, working closely with Venetian conservators, who often had the best of intentions but to whom restoration was little more than make-do-and-mend fabric repair, or pastiche overpainting of damaged masterpieces. In this area Ruskin makes it clear that successful conservation depends on a profound understanding of everything comprised in a given object, from the spirit of its age to the workaday artisan techniques involved in its construction.

Turning to his anti-Palladian diatribes, Ruskin firmly believed that Venice was a Gothic city, both in body and in spirit, and that Palladian *tours de force* like San Giorgio and the Redentore were impertinent interlopers, severely contaminating the integrity of the city. Gothic architecture was, for him, a form of collective worship, whereby everyone from the richest patron down to the jobbing stonemason worked together to create something that was both livable and a standing celebration of man's relationship with God. In his mind, the Gothic was essentially a continuation of the medieval way of thinking in which tradesmen and artisans could set up stall in the shadow of the cathedral or palace and feel that they were part of it. Classical architecture (and also the Baroque and the Rococo) were more about power and social division. He famously said that if you were to strip away the picturesque components of boats, boatmen, water, etc., the Palladian buildings in Venice would seem little more than provincial, civic edifices, hastily put together from Vitruvian copybooks; superficial advertisements of wealth and patronage. What he does not realise is how intense his appreciation of Palladio in fact was. He speaks longingly of that 'crimson on San Giorgio', the insistent classical starkness of the church's profile at long last softened and humanised for him by the palette of the setting sun. Finally it appeared as one of the most precious of Venice's eternal and elemental shapes and forms, as it also was for Turner and Monet, rather than a troublesome ideological emblem of a distant age.

Bearing Ruskin's prejudice in mind, my personal view is that Palladian, Neoclassical or Classical schemes usually work best on a blank slate in the countryside. In cities, this kind of building never really fits in unless it is part of a large and entirely homogenous scheme, like Belgravia in London or the Capitol in Washington, DC. These were both virgin sites when the buildings went up, and therefore the completed schemes did not and do not interfere with anything around them. And in a rural context, the Palladian approach works brilliantly: you typically find an untouched Arcadian wilderness at the periphery of a villa and its estate; the landscape leading from periphery to villa is progressively refined and tamed (lakes, judiciously planted copses and avenues of trees, a Dutch-style formal garden, and so on), finally culminating in the order and beauty of the house itself. It is an 18th-century way of looking at things, balancing Nature and Art. It does not sit so comfortably in an urban setting, where homogeneity, history and slow, progressive (and uninterrupted) expansion produce the most pleasing results. This is an age-old debate: the city as a living organism versus the city as a backdrop for further, immediate (and often discordant) emblems of change. Perhaps, if one has time, a second Gin and Tonic could be taken at Malcontenta on the mainland, having first visited Palladio's great country house masterpiece, the Villa Foscari, and one could meditate on why the style seems to work so much better here.

Palladian controversies aside, before leaving La Calcina and bidding what is always a fond and temporary farewell to Ruskin, both his passions and his prejudices, I invariably recall one of his most uplifting and liberating utterances: 'No true disciple of mine will ever be a "Ruskinian". He will follow not me, but the instincts of his own soul, and the guidance of its Creator.'

'...the friendly crowd of Venetians clustered on the jetty, a few of whom will have arrived in motorboats....'.

18. TAVERNA AL REMER

Taverna Al Remer is a superb bar-restaurant overlooking the Grand Canal and the Rialto. It would be difficult to contrive a more enjoyably 'Venetian' experience than this. To begin with, it is quite hard to find, a small network of alleys, courts and archways protecting it from the tidal wave of passing trade between Campo Goldoni and Ca' d'Oro. It is difficult to describe the pleasure to be had from taking a friend here for the first time. First, a trudge through crowded streets; then, an unpromising turn into what appears to be a dank, depressing alley leading nowhere; finally, a glimmer of light and a triumphant entry into one of the most attractive courtyards in Venice. Usually, the charm of the courtyard itself will distract the visitor's attention first; then he or she will catch sight of the jetty on the Grand Canal, and the view of the market and the Rialto Bridge. One might join the friendly crowd of Venetians clustered on the jetty, a few of whom will have arrived in motorboats which they moor alongside. Alternatively one might pause to admire the late-Romanesque well-head at the centre of the courtyard before venturing into the

The courtyard of Palazzo Lion Morosini, with the outdoor tables of Taverna Al Remer.

vaulted interior of the Taverna itself. Now is the time to order a bottle of Malvasia, an appropriate choice given the Peloponnesian antecedents of the grape and the Levantine meditations that will follow—and also a fitting reminder of the energetic entrepreneurial drive of the Venetian Republic which pretty much single-handedly created a lucrative pan-European market for this wine in various guises from the 16th century onwards. Malvasia is thought to have Greek roots and its name is probably a corruption of Monemvasia, the fortress-town on the coast of the Peloponnese where the Venetians had a trading post. The wine that would have been sent through Monemvasia in the 14th century would have been sweet. In England it was known as Malmsey. George, Duke of Clarence, the brother of King Edward IV, famously drowned in a butt of it, perhaps the most memorable thing to happen in any of Shakespeare's history plays. Today Malvasia is a dry white, the colour of polished brass, and in flavour can be pleasingly complex. It pairs perfectly with fish, so at Al Remer that is what I tend to order. My toast is to the Lion family, the 12th-century Venetian merchants who made this delightful setting possible.

A staple topic of conversation among Venetians and Venetophiles is the extent to which the early architecture of the city calls to mind the Levant, or indeed the 'East' at large. There is seldom any precise identification of exactly what is being called to mind, bar an agreeable but cloudy notion of Byzantium, or of Venetian footprints left in Cyprus or Croatia, or of a 'Moorish' influence ingested by some mysterious process in the early Middle Ages. The Corte del Remer, dominated by the Palazzo Lion Morosini, built in the late 13th century by the Lion family, belongs to that world. 'Eclectic' is a word architects often use to describe this *palazzo*. Al Remer is on its ground floor. The outdoor staircase, with surviving sections of Gothic trefoil balustrades, is one striking curiosity. Another, at the top of the stairs, is the enormous round-arched doorway, with its flanking pair of twin-lancet Venetian-Byzantine windows with moulded ogee lintels. Like many Venetian buildings, Palazzo Lion is a splendid example of how patrons and architects responded to the challenge of building within the comparatively restricted sites available in the city. The whole effect is beautiful, detailed on a remarkably small scale, resolutely theatrical and—dare one say it—cinematic in feel. More than this, though, the building and its courtyard offer specific echoes of the eastern Mediterranean location to which they owe their birth.

From the early 12th century until the Siege of Acre in 1291, Venetian trade expanded enormously in the Levant (literally the 'land of the sunrise'), the region that roughly corresponds to modern-day Israel, Jordan, Lebanon and Syria. Acre, a harbour city in the far north of what is now Israel, was then a thriving trading post, a Crusader stronghold, capital since 1191 of the Frankish Kingdom of Jerusalem.

Several Venetian merchant families, among them the Lion and the Zorzi, had settled in Acre, establishing a permanent expatriate community. These merchants brought their wives and families from Venice, built houses and palaces, cultivated farms and olive groves, enjoyed cordial relations with Muslims and fell in easily with the local lifestyle. This satisfactory state of affairs came to an abrupt end on 6th April, 1291, when the Mamluk Sultan, Al-Ashraf Khalil, arrived from Cairo, intent on capturing the city. In addition to an enormous army, drawn from as far afield as Tripoli, Hama and Damascus, he had also brought with him two enormous siege catapults, *Al-Mansuri* ('The Victorious') and *Al-Ghadiba* ('The Furious'). The Sultan's retinue pitched his *dhizil*, the scarlet tent of state, on a nearby hilltop, and the siege commenced. Despite spirited resistance from the Knights Templar and the arrival of reinforcements from England, Cyprus and Venice, Khalil's army breached the walls on 18th May and the Mamluk army poured into the city. Later, in June, Sultan Khalil rode triumphantly into Damascus, bringing with him 280 fettered prisoners. One of them was forced to carry an upended Frankish banner, and a spear festooned with the blood-matted hair of beheaded Crusader knights.

Among the (surprisingly high) number of those successfully evacuated from Acre were the Lion family, who had set sail for Venice before the walls were breached. On their return, they and other refugee families from the

Taverna Al Remer.

Kingdom of Jerusalem were ennobled, following a special decree passed by the Senate. The Lions celebrated their new status by building Palazzo Lion in Corte del Remer. Considering the nostalgia the family must have felt for their carefree days in Acre, it comes as no surprise that the building bears an uncanny resemblance to a place they knew and loved there, the cloister of the Hospital of St John. So Corte del Remer, as well as being an idyllic place to drink and think, is one of the most dramatic examples of local architecture bearing clear witness to the alternately prosperous and perilous adventures of expatriate Venetian merchants in the early days of the Republic.

19. CAFFÈ FLORIAN

In *The Wings of the Dove* (1902), Henry James describes Caffè Florian as 'a great social saloon, a smooth-floored, blue-roofed chamber of amenity'. Even in those days it was a venerable institution. It was opened in Piazza San Marco on 29th December 1720 as 'Alla Venezia Trionfante', but Venetians quickly took to nicknaming it after its genial founder, Floriano Francesconi, and the name has stuck ever since. Florian has moved with the times—in the best sense of that often highly dubious course of action—in particular becoming known as a promoter of contemporary art, a nod towards a famous dinner held here in 1893 that resulted in the foundation of the Venice Biennale.

Florian is a deceptive place, in fact much larger than one initially supposes. It is not obvious from the exterior, but inside there are six rooms to choose from: the Sala Cinese and Sala Orientale (Chinese and Oriental rooms), with 19th-century murals; the Sala degli Uomini Illustri ('Room of the Illustrious Men'), with portraits of ten Venetian luminaries ranging from the warrior-doge Enrico Dandolo to the patrician composer Benedetto Marcello; the Sala delle

Stagioni ('Room of the Seasons'), sometimes called the Hall of Mirrors, where looking-glasses multiply the interior, the Piazza, the Basilica and indeed oneself into an infinitely repeated collage of the present moment; the Sala Liberty ('Art Nouveau Room'), a pretty salon added in 1920 to mark Florian's bicentenary; and my favourite of all, the Sala del Senato ('Senate Hall'). It was here, at a dinner in 1893, that Riccardo Selvatico, Venetian playwright and sometime mayor of Venice, first had the idea of staging a revolving exhibition of international art. That year Florian hosted Venice's first Esposizione Internazionale d'Arte Contemporanea, a project whose success led to the first iteration of the Venice Biennale in 1895. So this is where it all began, and appropriately enough, the ceiling of the Senate Hall has, at its centre, an allegorical painting by Giacomo Casa optimistically entitled *Civilisation Educating the Nations*.

As to food and drink, Florian's own soft-centred, candy-coloured macaroons are delicious, and it is hard to find better examples of *zaletti*, buttery biscuits with raisins. And of course there is a Florian signature dish, the *tiramisù*. I find the best accompaniment for any—or preferably all—of these is one of Florian's own tea blends, the Venice 1720, a superb Orange Pekoe enlivened with cinnamon, carnation petals and nutmeg. Unless one makes the effort to brew tea properly, it will not taste right. Orange Pekoe is a black tea and to get it to yield its true copper colour it should

be steeped for about three minutes in water that is close to boiling. It is best drunk without milk or sugar. The addition of a little fresh lemon is admissible.

All this comes at a terrific price of course, particularly if the Florian orchestra is playing, when a surcharge might be added to the bill. But I have seldom heard anyone complain about the prices here. Beautiful and unashamedly sensual *pâtisserie* at this level is happily devoured by a broad range of clients, from CEOs to student travellers, from seasoned lechers to demure maiden aunts. It may be that the frequent cameo appearances of Giacomo Casanova in the branding are partly responsible for this.

There have been plenty of other famous Florian regulars over the years, of course, from the inevitable Byron, Goethe and Proust to Fauré, A.E. Housman and Joseph Brodsky. In *Watermark*, Brodsky's classic meditation on Venice and Venetian life, the author finds himself in need of a drink and heads towards Florian at closing time on a chill winter's night (it was one of Brodsky's notable idiosyncrasies that he always chose to visit Venice in winter). On looking into one of the tall windows in the colonnade that had not yet been boarded up by the waiters, he imagines that time has transported Florian back to some halcyon point in the mid-1950s. He presents an imaginary tableau composed of four poets: W.H. Auden, Chester Kallman, Cecil Day-Lewis and Stephen Spender, seated near the window at a table laden

Orange Pekoe tea (and a rogue Negroni) at Caffè Florian.

with a 'Kremlin of drinks and tea-pots'. It is an arresting image, not so much for the assembled company but more because it typifies so accurately the uncanny sense one often has in Venice of reliving, possibly even being allowed to participate in, the vanished past. The illusions thrown back by the mirrors in Florian's *Sala delle Stagioni* are every bit as powerful as Brodsky's tableau, and every bit as fragile.

My own such Brodskyan moment usually comes in spring, not winter. When sitting outside in the sunny Piazza I often imagine a solitary A.E. Housman occupying a table nearby, gazing at the Campanile:

Caffè Florian, Sala Orientale.

Andrea, fare you well;
  Venice, farewell to thee.
The tower that stood and fell
  is not rebuilt in me.'

This, on Housman's part, was no ornamental or forced poetic reference to the collapse of the bell-tower in 1902 and its subsequent reconstruction but rather a reflection on the terrible moment in Housman's life when he decided, clearly and resolutely, that after twenty-five years of annual visits, Venice no longer held anything for him. Such disillusionment would surely be a terrible fate for any Venetophile. At all events it befell Housman, possibly as a result of difficulties in his relationship with his gondolier, Andrea, and all the other peripheral problems occasioned by unrequited love and intensifying self-doubt. As often with the fastidiously private Housman, one does not wish to pry. The quatrain quoted here, from *More Poems*, published in the year of the poet's death (1936), more than speaks for itself.

But let us not repine. One afternoon, as I was brooding over my Orange Pekoe in Florian's Sala del Senato, an immaculately clad and coiffed young tourist took a compact mirror from her Chanel handbag and used it to scrutinise, very studiously, the allegory on the ceiling. There is hope.

20. ROSA SALVA

Rosa Salva is a friendly and well-known *pasticceria* in Campo Santi Giovanni e Paolo (San Zanipolo in Venetian dialect). The Rosa Salva enterprise is primarily a catering company and has been a mainstay of entertaining in Venice since the 1870s, when Andrea Rosa established what he called his *trattoria itinerante*, 'roving *trattoria*', supplying banquets to the Venetian nobility at their palaces in town and their villas on the banks of the Brenta Canal, where he became a familiar sight, delivering his wares in the early morning by horse-drawn barge. Six generations on, the business is still thriving. Indeed, if you are a regular visitor to Venice and of a lazy disposition, it is worth getting to know the Rosa Salva shop in Calle Fiubera near Piazza San Marco. Here one can order a three-course takeaway 'banquet' for more or less the same price as it would cost to put the whole thing together from the supermarket or the stalls of the Rialto. Rosa Salva is also excellent for the purpose of assembling picnic hampers for trips to the Lido and beyond. As regards the *pasticceria* in Campo Santi Giovanni e Paolo, it is a perfect spot for a pot

20. ROSA SALVA

The Rosa Salva shopfront facing Campo Santi Giovanni e Paolo.

of tea and, on especially cold days, a hot glass of Punch Arancio, an orange-flavoured liqueur. To go with them I will order a plate of *cantucci*, almond biscuits, or *esse buranei*, the S-shaped butter cookies from Burano, entirely happy to commit the Venetian heresy of dunking them in the Punch, as opposed to in a traditional *vin santo*. And as I look across the *campo* towards Venice's sprawling main hospital, I invariably raise this warming libation to the memory of Dr Giuseppe Jona, who was arguably the foremost hero of Venetian Jewish resistance against the Third Reich.

Plots to oust Mussolini from power led to his deposition in the summer of 1943. An armistice with the Allies was signed in early September. Nazi Germany acted swiftly, rapidly occupying and formally annexing much of Italy. Mussolini was recalled and set at the head of a puppet government headquartered on Lake Garda. The agents of the Reich then took steps to fulfil their ultimate aims. Less than ten days after the armistice had officially been announced, the leader of the Jewish community in Venice took his own life. How had this come about? And why is Rosa Salva on Campo Santi Giovanni e Paolo an appropriate place to raise a glass to this heroic man?

Giuseppe Jona was born in 1866. He trained as a physician and soon established himself in the anatomy and pathology department of Venice's Civil Hospital. Later, following the battle of Caporetto in WWI, he offered his services as consultant to the overwhelmed military hospitals. For the schemes that he put in place he won fulsome praise from the Ministry of the Interior. In the early 1920s he was elected president of the Ateneo Veneto, Venice's academy of sciences and the arts. When Italy introduced its Race Laws in 1938, designed to bring the country into line with Nazi Germany, Jona was over seventy and though he had already retired from the hospital, he was expelled from the Ateneo and lost his doctor's license. Instead he took on the role of *de facto* leader of the Jewish community, providing valuable

Plaque to Giuseppe Jona in Campo del Ghetto Nuovo.
Through the window is the Ba'Ghetto restaurant (p. 109).

A glass of warm Punch Arancio with accompanying *esse* biscuits.

support to the now elderly and blind Rabbi of Venice, Adolfo Ottolenghi, an assumption of responsibility all the more remarkable because Jona was by no means a devout, practising Jew. After the German occupation of 1943, he elected to stay in Venice rather than attempt to escape. He was summoned to the Prefecture on the Grand Canal and ordered to hand over a list of all the Jews remaining in the city. Jona calmly assured the authorities he would produce the relevant documents within three days, a precious fragment of time he bought dearly and used well. He spent those three days burning every piece of evidence he could find in the Ghetto archives. Having done this, he set his affairs in order, made a will, then committed suicide by giving himself a lethal injection of morphine. This extraordinary act of self-sacrifice is thought to have saved the lives of some 1,400 people. Today, there is a commemorative plaque to Jona in the Venice Ghetto. One of the wards in the Ospedale Civile, Venice's main hospital which stretches between Campo Santi Giovanni e Paolo and the lagoon, is named after Giuseppe Jona. It is looking across at that hospital, which can still be entered through the magnificent hall of the ex-Scuola di San Marco, that I raise my cup of tea and my glass of Punch Arancio to one of the greatest heroes of the city.

Enoteca Al Volto.

21. ENOTECA AL VOLTO

Enoteca Al Volto is a traditional Venetian *bàcaro*, an old-fashioned bar serving Veneto wines and a huge selection of the famous Venetian *cicchetti*, little morsels of cured meat, grilled vegetables or fish served on bread or on plump little mattresses of polenta. The word *bàcaro* carries with it a pleasing archaic resonance. This is a 'tavern', a place of low ceilings and thick walls, where people come not to eat but to drink and converse (and possibly conspire). *Cicchetti* are available to ward off inebriation, but sit-down dinners are not traditionally on offer. In today's Venice, however, a place whose transient population far outnumbers the residents, *bàcari* are increasingly bowing to visitor demand and offering meals in their back rooms. In the snug inner chamber at Al Volto, you can enjoy Venetian classics such as *fegato all veneziana* (liver cooked with onions), *sarde in saor* (sardines marinated in onions and a sweet and sour sauce), and an ocean of fried and grilled fish.

In fine weather, Al Volto puts a few tables outside in the narrow *calle*. This is where I like to sit, to raise a glass to the reigning spirit of this little corner of Venice. The Grand Canal is very close. If you walk to the end of the *calle* and turn right, you come to Palazzo Loredan. On its further corner (Calle del Carbon) is a plaque commemorating the achievements of Elena Cornaro Piscopia, among the first women to graduate from a university, and the first woman ever to graduate with a doctorate in Philosophy, from the University of Padua in 1678. Palazzo Loredan, now Venice's Town Hall (*Municipio*), was her birthplace and former home. The plaque is directly opposite the Coop supermarket, an accident prompting the queasy thought that for many of us—men and women alike—no amount of scholarly endeavour can silence the urgent call of domestic tyranny.

Elena was a child prodigy and by the time she was seven she had earned the nickname *Septilingue Oraculum*, the 'Oracle in Seven Languages': in addition to her native Italian, she had also mastered Latin, Greek, Hebrew, Arabic, Spanish and French. In her teens she took a great interest in astronomy, physics and linguistics, and in her spare time she devoted herself to music, playing her own compositions on the harpsichord, the harp and the violin. Despite this glittering trajectory, it took careful advocacy from Carlo Rinaldini and Felice Rotondi, her tutors in Philosophy and Theology respectively, to persuade the University of Padua to recognise her achievements. Elena was originally set on gaining a doctorate in Theology, but this was fiercely opposed by Cardinal Gregorio Barbarigo, the Bishop of Padua, on the

The laurel-garlanded plaque to Elena Cornaro Piscopia, on the side of the *palazzo* where she was born in 1646.

grounds of her sex. In the end, a compromise was found in Philosophy, and on 25th May 1678 she attended her degree ceremony. In an unusual departure from convention, Padua's cathedral had been chosen as the venue, as none of the university halls could accommodate the enormous crowd who had come to witness Elena's triumph. The ceremony began with a public *viva voce*, lasting an hour, in which Elena confidently expanded in Latin on the various passages from Aristotle randomly fired at her by the examiners.

Following the standing ovation at the end, her old friend and tutor Rinaldini had the pleasure of investing her with her doctorate. He crowned her with a laurel wreath, placed a ring on her finger, and set the ermine mantle of Padua University squarely on her shoulders. Sadly, within a few months, the university altered its statutes so as to forbid any further female graduations. It was not until 1732 that an Italian woman was once again to graduate from a university: Laura Bassi at Bologna.

There are few known portraits of Elena. Perhaps the best known shows a quiet, thoughtful young woman with delicate features, dark eyes and curly hair. Seated in an armchair upholstered in rich crimson, she wears an austere black dress that perfectly offsets (as fashion writers might say) the luxurious ermine mantle proclaiming her degree. In her left hand she holds a copy of Aristotle, and with her right she points to an astrolabe, glimmering in the background. A more triumphalist image of her, demonstrating how far-reaching her fame has proved to be, can be seen in the superb Cornaro Window (1906), in the Thompson Memorial Library at Vassar College. This faux-devotional stained-glass tribute shows Elena perched, Madonna-like, in a pulpit in Padua Cathedral, surrounded by admiring, if not adoring, ranks of scholars. Above her, in place of saints or Evangelists, are seven vignettes featuring personifications of Grammar, Dialectic, Music, Philosophy, Astronomy,

Elena Cornaro Piscopia (1646-84), in a portrait from the Biblioteca Ambrosiana in Milan, with a volume of Aristotle in her hand and an astrolabe at her side.

Medicine and Theology. She never married: at an early age she had taken a vow of chastity, in order to concentrate on her studies and avoid the supermarket checkout queue. She died aged of tuberculosis thirty-eight, having devoted the later years of her life to scholarship and ministering to the poor.

What I drink, when I toast Elena Cornaro, is Valpolicella, a wine made on the east shore of Lake Garda, near Verona. It has been traded and consumed in various forms in Venice since the 8th century and it comes in a number of manifestations from Classico and Classico Superiore to its finest incarnations: Amarone, Ripasso and Recioto.

Amarone is a velvety, garnet-coloured paradise of a wine that can reach up to 17 degrees of strength, though normally it hovers around 13 or 14. Ripasso is a complex wine made by a technique that involves a secondary fermentation induced by the addition of grape skins left over from the making of Amarone. Recioto is a variant with a distinctive sweetness, achieved by partially drying the grapes prior to fermentation. Comparing Valpolicella wines is always interesting: ideally, if time and budget allows, I like to treat myself to a measure of Classico and another of Amarone, served in ample glasses that could contain a lagoon or even an ocean of wine if you so wished. It is a conscious attempt on my part to mimic and overturn the hourglasses that were once used as timers for interminable sermons up until the 17th century.

22. SOTTOVENTO

Sottovento is that rare thing in Venice, a 'hidden gem'. Many hidden gems here are in reality rather self-proclaiming: 'I am off the beaten track!' they cry, Garbo-like, with megaphones. The small bar is tricky to find, set back some way from the main drag of Murano's Rivalonga. Once you do find it, the absence of tourists can seem quite startling. Sottovento has a faithful local clientèle, particularly in evidence in the early evening after work. The floor of the bar, recently designed and installed by a local architect, is quite remarkable. It is paved with circular slices of superannuated *bricole*, the stout timber piles you see in tightly hugging groups of three in the lagoon, marking the principal waterways.

When I come here I tend to order the 'San Daniele' platter of cold cuts and a Spritz Hugo. This wonderful hybrid of the popular drink is made with Prosecco, elderflower cordial and fresh mint. It cools the body after a visit to one of Murano's glass furnaces. It is a pleasure to watch the bartender pluck the mint from a row of vases on the secret, and very charming, terrace at the back of the bar. It is the

Spritz Hugo at Sottovento.

SPRITZ HUGO

Ingredients: Prosecco and elderflower cordial in a relationship of about 7 parts to 1. A dash of soda water. Fresh mint leaves and a slice of lemon to garnish.

Method: Pour the elderflower cordial into a glass on top of a few cubes of ice. Add the Prosecco and then a top of soda water. Garnish with a sprig or two of fresh mint and half a slice of lemon.

ultimate little retreat. If there is space there, I settle down to consider the development of the Murano glassblower's art from the 15th century onwards. This was as much a triumph of science as it was of art, having all the mystery and ritual of alchemy but with little of the attendant disappointment. One contemplates the failed experiments and landmark eureka moments that led Angelo Barovier's perfection of *cristallo*, a glass so light that a mere whisper of wind could set it trembling, chiming and singing.

If Angelo Barovier was the wizard of exquisite drinking vessels and vases, the prince of chandeliers was undoubtedly a later master, Giuseppe Briati (1686–1772). Every multi-branched floral extravaganza you see is easily traceable back to the workshops of Briati, who popularised the distinctive design known as *ciocche* (literally, 'bouquets'). Since 1291, Venetian glass manufacturers had been legally obliged to operate their furnaces in Murano, to eliminate the risk of fire in the city centre. Briati had the rare distinction of having been permitted by the Council of Ten, in 1732, to move his operation back into central Venice: his chandelier monopoly had so triumphantly outshone the efforts of his Muranese competitors that he and his workforce soon became victims of nefarious acts of sabotage and eventually death threats. The Council of Ten, mindful of Briati's significant contribution to the local economy, were happy to protect him. Despite his persecution at the hands of the jealous *muranesi*, and the enforced 'exile' that ensued, Briati was generous, and ploughed a portion of his considerable profits back into the island. He built a beautiful oratory, and within its foundation endowed a hospice to accommodate twelve indigent widows of glassblowers. In some ways there could be a case for appointing Briati, an unashamed decorator, the unofficial patron saint of the Venetian glass industry. Modern manufacturers have much to thank him for as they struggle to reinvent themselves and market their products in

22. SOTTOVENTO

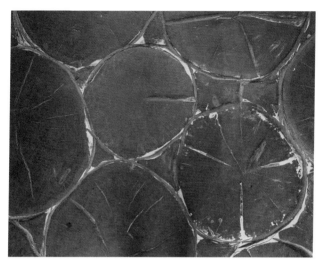

Detail of the floor of Sottovento, made from sections of *bricole*, the wooden posts used to mark navigable channels in the Venetian lagoon.

an increasingly competitive landscape. Thankfully for them, the international hospitality industry goes from strength to strength: there will always be demand for these lurid, hothouse-grown, chandelier-orchids in hotels, conference centres and casinos from Dubai to Manila, from Las Vegas to Limassol and beyond.

And there will always be demand for pretty knick-knacks. Among the many unconsidered trifles one can snap up are Murano glass beads. These are no more than frippery today,

Murano glass beads, piled in a heap like boiled sweets. Pretty trinkets that once had significant bartering value.

but there was a time when they were valuable currency, known as *conterie*. According to an account published in 1847 by Domenico Bussolin, himself a Murano glass-worker, the beads were eagerly sought by countries as far afield as China and not only did Venice trade in them herself; she also sold them to the Spanish, Portuguese, French and British, for use as barter to buy gold dust, gum arabic, wood, furs and spices. Along with these commodities, however, glass beads were also traded for human lives. As glass manufacturers outside Venice perfected their technologies and improved their product—despite Murano's efforts to keep its workings a mystery—Venice saw her monopoly on glassware steadily slipping away. The beads, however, kept their value and large quantities of them were supplied to Britain to be traded for slaves. And thus did wickedness become embodied in the prettiest and seemingly most inconsequential of artefacts.

A key figure in the recent history of Murano glass was neither a Venetian nor a glassblower, though his name is synonymous with some of the finest products to emerge from Murano over the last century. Paolo Venini was born at Lake Como in 1895 and fell in love with Venice while he was stationed there during the First World War. He studied law for a while in Milan, before returning to Venice in 1921 when, with no prior business or management experience whatsoever, he bought the Andrea Rioda glass furnaces on Murano. Despite several quickly extinguished partnerships and a few shattered illusions, by the 1930s the Venini name was firmly established as one of the most innovative enterprises on Murano. At the loftier aesthetic level, Venini began to work with carefully chosen artists and designers, including Napoleone Martinuzzi, Carlo Scarpa and Fulvio Bianconi. Though these partnerships generated a series of beautiful and valuable objects, Venini was nonetheless mindful of the need to exploit the lower end of the market. He saw no reason why cheaper objects should be any less beautiful than the one-off creations at the high end of the spectrum. This may seem a tritely obvious policy, until one pauses to consider how, in general, cheap Murano glass is often embodied in gaudy trinkets or embarrassing keepsakes: the gurning miniature clown, the lazily approximated horse or lion, the bilious ashtray in acid green or pustulent scarlet. A perfect example of Venini's aesthetic in action was his collaboration with Carlo Scarpa, who designed a wide range of small bowls, vases or glasses, often in single colours— glorious Venetian blues, eau-de-nils and russets—a shining palette that Scarpa had reincarnated from the early days of Murano glass. Though expensive now, these Venini/Scarpa collaborations were intentionally affordable in the day.

As I sit in Sottovento, I raise my glass to the remaining glassblowers of Murano, greatly reduced in number these days, as few young people are attracted by such a physically punishing profession. Nevertheless, against all the odds, the industry survives.

23. CAFFÈ ROSSO

Caffè Rosso is a long-established bar in Campo Santo Margherita, 'bohemian' in the sense that it stays open very late (unlike most bars in Venice) and is patronised by undergraduates from Ca'Foscari, the university of Venice. The deconsecrated church of Santa Margherita is both a lecture hall and the venue for degree ceremonies. As the evening wears on, the *campo* begins to fill up with its cast of stock characters: Italian-Americans from Youngstown, Ohio singing *O sole mio*; the Dravidian rose-vendor with his beseeching eyes and sad, petrol station blooms; and Aldo the Hippy performing his inevitable Beatles medley. My drink of choice here is the Mojito. Not very Venetian, one could argue, but very much a student cocktail and the Cuban rum that is its key component is also of some significance—at least, it has some tangential political resonance that I hope will become clear later. As to the accompanying snack, I favour the *tramezzino*—again, a surprisingly political item. This plain white, triangular sandwich owes its name to Gabriele d'Annunzio, who coined it in 1925 at the Caffè Mulassano in Turin: '*Ci vorrebbe un altro di quei golosi tramezzini,*' he is

'Caffè' on Campo Santa Margherita (the 'Rosso' speaks for itself).

said to have murmured, after tasting a sandwich of bread and butter with anchovies. His coinage makes use of the architectural term *tramezzo*, an 'object falling between two other objects'. Later, in the thirties, D'Annunzio's neologism was taken up by Achille Starace, a Mussolini henchman tasked with promoting nationalist ideology. Starace added *tramezzino* to a growing list of Italian words intended as patriotic replacements for British or American ones. Some, for example *pallavolo* (volleyball) and *autorimessa* (garage), caught on; others did not, a ludicrous example being *coda di gallo* (rooster's tail) for cocktail.

MOJITO

Ingredients: 2 parts fresh lime juice, 1 part rum, 1 part soda, sugar syrup to taste, plenty of fresh mint leaves (at least ten).

Method: Pour the fresh lime juice into a highball glass, add the sugar and mint leaves and crush. Fill the glass with crushed ice, pour the rum on top and mix well. Garnish with more fresh mint.

For quite unusual reasons, Caffè Rosso is an apt place to reflect on all this. It is difficult to imagine, as one sits here contentedly, that this gentle bohemian *campo* was, in the 1920s, the scene of violent street battles between Blackshirts and the Bolshevik left. At the south end of the square (to your right if you are sitting outside Caffè Rosso) is the building of the old fur traders' guild (adorned, perhaps appropriately, with a relief of the Madonna of Mercy, shielding the defenceless under a vast and voluminous cloak). Just here, where a fishmonger now sets up his stall, two protestors were killed by police in one of these skirmishes. Looking back further in time, to before the First World War, a curious instance of Venetian civic pride was born in the Albergo Capon, the small hotel directly opposite Caffè Rosso. It was emblematic of the spirit that later drove the anti-Fascist insurrectionists and as such well worth recalling.

In the first decade of the last century, the *albergo* was owned by a genial, energetic (and extremely fat) man called Capon, whose vast bulk and legendary gluttony led to his nickname Pastasutta, Venetian dialect for *pastasciutta*, a term used to refer to any staple type of dry pasta boiled in water. Ever since Venice joined the Kingdom of Italy in 1866— and continuing to this day—there have been secessionist movements pleading the case for its detachment. *Evviva San Marco*! Venice for Venetians! *Pax tibi Marce*! are some

Campo Santa Margherita is a popular place for demonstrations and rallies. Ever since Venice joined the Kingdom of Italy in 1866 there have been secessionist movements pleading the case for its detachment. Here a crowd gathers under the banners of one such separatist party, Indipendenza Veneta.

of the heroic battle cries one might still hear at the end of a bibulous evening. In 1909, Pastasutta took this ever-simmering separatist tendency a stage further by declaring Campo Santa Margherita and the surrounding district a Republic. The 'Repubblica di Santa Margherita' quickly gained traction, with Pastasutta organising weekly lunches and dinners attended by a broad spectrum of local society, including dockers, porters, gondoliers, undergraduates, professors, poets, artists and drunks. These events were extremely popular until they were suspended during the Austrian bombardment of Venice in the First World War. Following the war, with Mussolini's star on the rise, the dining club and its headquarters at Albergo Capon were revived but as Mussolini's regime gained momentum, Venetian society became polarised into left and right factions. It thus became the custom for the Left to gather at Albergo Capon while the Right congregated opposite in Caffè Rosso (the irony of the colour did not go unnoted; today my drink of choice there is Cuban rum). I should add that if you sit outside Caffè Rosso, and if you do choose to order a *tramezzino*, beware of the seagulls. I have seen one deftly bear away the contents of an entire plate, before the waiter had even set it down.

24. BAR CAFFÈ REDENTORE

Bar Caffè Redentore is a pleasant little bar near Campo Santo Stefano. It occupies a corner site, just before the bridge leading to Campiello Feltrina, from where the long and well-worn tramp to San Marco begins. I tend to see this little place as a valuable marker, the last watering hole in this stretch of the *sestiere* before the price-hikes begin in earnest. It is also one of the last-remaining authentic Venetian bars in a city increasingly given over to serving a population that does not live here, who have come here on holiday and who wish to linger lazily over long drinks, not stand at a zinc-topped bar and knock back a hasty, restorative *espresso* or a miniature shot of something stronger.

The *cicchetteria* at Al Redentore is generous and good: large slices of crispy bread, with fragrant *baccalà*, or *sopressa* (slices of Veneto salami) with sun-dried tomatoes. There are tables outside, ranged along the narrow Fondamenta della Malvasia Vecchia, alongside the canal. This *fondamenta*, running at a right-angle to the main drag towards San Marco, is by no means a major thoroughfare, so this is a perfect place to relax. Here, an *ombra* could be had for one euro fifty at the time of writing. This is also a place where one can order a *spritzino*, a mini-Spritz in a small glass costing around two euros. The *spritzino* is very much a Venetian construct, something you will never see on a menu but which can be ordered in most small-scale bars.

Another drink one can ask for at Al Redentore is the *pallina*. A very Venetian tradition, it is a member of the Spritz family but much less elaborate: a simple, down-in-one pick-me-up, its name translating literally 'little ball' or 'marble', a colloquial term for the small wine glass or goblet in which it is typically served. With a *pallina*, the fripperies of ice, soda and fruit garnish are abandoned, leaving one with a 50/50 mix consisting of a workmanlike slug of liqueur and a slurp

---

PALLINA

Ingredients: 1 part Select, 1 part still white wine.
A dash of soda if required. No ice, no garnish.

Method: Pour the Select into a small glass.
Add the wine. Stir briefly or agitate with a
buzz of soda.

24. BAR CAFFÈ REDENTORE

Two *palline*, as served at Redentore, in small shot glasses placed on the wooden counter below the serving hatch.

of still white wine. A top of soda can be added too. The *Pallina* is a staple in most down-to-earth, vernacular *bàcari*—and the reason I like to order one from time to time is because I would like to think that it is a tradition that can stay alive. At Al Redentore, it lingers. Many bars in Venice, however, will not now agree to serve a *pallina*: their time is better used serving more expensive drinks.

If one were minded to follow the workmanlike pleasures of the *pallina* with a plutocratic *aperitivo* at the Gritti Palace (*p. 137*), then it would be essential to pause on the way and inspect the exuberant Baroque façade of Santa Maria del Giglio. No edifying or admonitory scriptural friezes are presented here, no devotional iconography to warm the hearts of the faithful. Instead, one is confronted by what is arguably one of the least Christian church façades in Christendom, commissioned and paid for by the great Venetian admiral Antonio Barbaro (d. 1679), whose statue dominates the scheme (at the top) alongside depictions of his four brothers (in the register below). They are attended not by biblical patriarchs or saints, but by allegorical figures representing Fame, Wisdom, Honour and Virtue. At ground level, at the feet of the six main columns, are striking

Relief of Corfu Town on the façade of Santa Maria del Giglio.
Mandraki harbour is shown complete with two galleons. The huge Spianada parade ground appears to have a windmill at one end.

A *pallina* in the traditional tulip-shaped mini goblet.

relief maps carved deep into slabs of Istrian marble, each commemorating a location at which Barbaro and his family played a significant role: Crete, Corfu, Padua, Rome, Split and Zadar. I have often seen children marvelling at the maps—it is a delight to observe them running their fingers along the exquisite grooves and protruberances of the petrified cities, knowing and caring nothing of the dynastic triumphs that were enacted there. The only church façade in Venice that comes close to the theatrical self-celebration of Giglio is that of San Moisè, nearby, bearing depictions and memorials of the Cypriot traders Vincenzo and Girolamo Fini, who like Barbaro commissioned their own private scheme. In a city that sternly forbade the erecting of public statues of individuals, lest self-aggrandisement take precedence over serving the interests of the Republic, men of mark found other ways to tell the world about their exploits. One might add that it is not only God who fails to be assigned a slice of Barbaro's extravagant Baroque cake; the Venetian Republic fares no better: the Santa Maria del Giglio façade lacks any imagery that overtly refers to Venice rather than merely to the exploits of the Barbaro family in her service. There are no bookish lions, no attendant patron saints, nor even the slightest nod to St Mark the Evangelist in this delightfully self-proclaiming scheme. Indeed, in an inspired choreographic *tour de force* that is easy to miss, the architect, Giuseppe Sardi, has positioned the statue of Fame on the top left of the façade in such a way that she blows her trumpet in the direction of the Grand Canal. Thus the fanfare for Barbaro's triumphs has echoed across the waters for centuries, over the lagoon and out across the sea, dying somewhere amid the Eastern Mediterranean relics of Venice's fallen empire.

25. KIOSK LE COCCINELLE

Life in Venice is by no means all Ruskin, romance and *Ripasso*, as many commentators would have you believe. There is the insistent nitty-gritty to be dealt with, the sourcing of kitchen equipment, groceries and other household supplies, electrical gadgets, sheets and curtains, power tools, even. And few of these are consistently available at a reasonable price in the vicinity of San Marco. There used to be men in Venice who would barely stray beyond the boundaries of their native *campo*, venturing out in their Sunday best only at Easter time or for the feast of the Salute. I would enjoy being one of these, but occasionally one has to take a trip further afield, to the retail complex in Marghera. I treat these trips as a kind of adventure. The complex is the size of several sports stadia, and although I have come there solely for the purpose of buying, say, a refrigerator, I nonetheless feel the urge to stock up on things that one simply cannot buy in the historic centre. I load my trolley with a random selection of essentials from the various shops, all housed in enormous concrete boxes. On the way out, I greet a nonagenarian local resident, Mario, who sits

Marghera viewed across the water. Its oil refinery and curving pipeline bridge are a familiar sight.

dazed in the jazzy cafeteria. He is one of the few people who remembers when 'all this was fields'.

The refrigerator comes from SME, a basilica of white goods, curtain-rails, garden pergolas, watering cans and decking. I cannot carry it back with me; it will eventually arrive in Venice on a boat. I head back to Mestre, and from there by bus to Piazzale Roma, disembarking into an unwarrantably grey and drizzly afternoon, the holiday over. To prolong it ever such a little, I head to the refreshment kiosk Le Coccinelle. It is my favourite stop for a celebratory drink on arriving at Piazzale Roma, the last place reachable by motor traffic before the waterborne idyll begins. This terminus is filled with groups of arriving or departing tourists, as well as Venetians going about their daily business, cursing the late arrival of a bus, running for a train or a *vaporetto*. Le Coccinelle is no more than a shack overlooking the busy Piazzale. It is not the sort of place that tourists go to. Its clientèle is largely Venetian: workmen waiting for mainland mates, lovers waiting for their *terraferma* partners. But it provides a fascinating vantage point, enabling one to see the surprise, ecstasy or bewilderment of tourists who

Kiosk Le Coccinelle.

Early morning fog envelops Piazzale Roma.
A day that calls for a hot chocolate at Kiosk Le Coccinelle.

disembark from the airport bus. Carpaccio might equally well document these questing, anxious faces. Where is the boat? How much are the taxis? Is there a bank near here? Is there a place for children? These quickly merge with another stream of tourists, who have arrived at Santa Lucia railway station. They cross Santiago Calatrava's once glistening but now fogged and dilapidated glass bridge, bringing them into Piazzale Roma. With each succeeding wave of new arrivals there is a steady rumble, rising to a roar, of a thousand suitcase wheels over glass, cement and tarmac, counterpointed by the businesslike growling and rattling of buses and trams.

Unlikely as it may seem, a point of interest in Piazzale Roma is the multi-storey carpark, designed by Eugenio Miozzi (1889–1979), usually celebrated as a bridge builder (the Accademia Bridge is his, as is the one at the Scalzi, directly opposite the railway station). When he completed the Piazzale Roma project in the 1930s it was much praised as the largest car park of its type in Europe. Time permitting, it is worth making a pilgrimage to its top level, just as you would visit the bell-towers of San Marco or San Giorgio Maggiore for the views. It offers a complete panorama of Venice: the mainland and road-rail bridge in one direction and the beckoning jewel box of the historic centre in the other. One pauses to reflect that the bridge to the mainland is not in fact a single bridge, but an amalgamation of two. The railway bridge was built in 1846 during the Austrian occupation, and it was not

until the 1930s that a road bridge was built alongside it. This too was designed by Eugenio Miozzi.

When one leaves the swirling interface of Piazzale Roma behind and heads into the city's quiet backwaters, however, one might be thankful that one of Miozzi's most ambitious projects never saw the light of day. If he had had his way, all of Venice's major islands, including the Lido, would have been interconnected by road and rail bridges. There was a fierce backlash against these proposals, led by groups from both Venice and abroad, collectively known as the *antipontisti*, the anti-bridge brigade. At Le Coccinelle, where the drizzle seems to call for hot chocolate, I drink as much to Miozzi's failure as to his engineering genius. Hot chocolate, one might think, has nothing whatever Venetian about it. But one can find a Venetian angle everywhere, if one knows where to look. It is said that Casanova had his own special recipe, which involved mixing cocoa powder with aphrodisiacs. This he would feed to his would-be conquests. At Le Coccinelle, they mix their cocoa with nothing more stimulating than milk and a little sugar. The result is entirely satisfactory.

26. TORCELLO

I love grappa. I first fell in love with it when a friend and I stayed on in Venice for a few days at the end of an Art History course. Our teacher gave us stern advice before he left. 'There are three things you must not do,' he said. 'Do not go to Harry's Bar; do not go to the Lido; and under no circumstances drink grappa.' I will not trouble you with an account of how we spent that first and precious evening of freedom. But I have been drinking grappa ever since.

Grappa is a clean and fiery spirit. It is made by distilling the skins and pips and stalks that are left over during the winemaking process, after the grapes have been crushed and their juice extracted. I have found that there are two grappa universes to explore, both of them rewarding. The first is very much of the street. In the Rialto Market, soon after sunrise on a Saturday morning, rubbing shoulders with gruff porters, one might try a *rasentin*, made by pouring a dash of cleansing spirit into the dregs of one's empty coffee cup and knocking it back. Then there is the completely different world enshrined in Poli Distillerie, a luxurious small shop in Campiello Feltrina, between Campo Santo

One of the finest emporia in Venice: the Poli grappa store in Campiello della Feltrina, *sestiere* of San Marco.

Stefano and Piazza San Marco. Poli has been making grappa since 1898, near the town of Bassano, about 70km northwest of Venice. The full name of the town is Bassano del Grappa, and though it happens to be the heartland of Italian grappa-making, its name in fact derives from Monte Grappa, the mountain that looms above it. Grappa the liqueur takes its name from the Latin word for grape.

It should be said straight away that Poli's is not a bar: one cannot sit there and amiably quaff grappa. But one can purchase some perfect examples of the distiller's art. The Cleopatra Moscato Oro, for instance, an extraordinarily sensual nectar proclaiming pineapple, mango and mandarin, sufficient to reduce even the sternest Mark Antony to soft but urgent libertinage. Or the exquisite Due Barili, with its insistent undertones of chocolate and hazelnut, aged for nine years in massive old casks of French oak that had once contained Spanish sherry, bringing to Venice the distant call of the *duende* or the sprightly rhythms of Domenico Scarlatti that once rang out in the palaces of La Granja, Aranjuez and El Escorial. Alternatively there is the Poli Barrique, a distillation of which the family is justly proud, an extravaganza of vanilla, coffee, liquorice and chocolate, recalling the amorous confusion of a night at the *Ridotto*. Or how about the Bassano Venti-Quattro Carati, nicknamed the 'Black Panther' by its devotees, who relish the seductive moment of cream and cashew before the native raw spirit springs forth with a terrific and unexpected bite. Possibly Jacopo Poli's greatest triumph, however, is La Première, distilled in barrels obtained after years of careful diplomacy from Château Pauillac. With its Francophone echoes of the Médoc, of marzipan and candied fruit, it is just as much an *eau-de-vie* as it is a grappa.

To enjoy my grappa, I first equip myself with a picnic of fragrant bread from the Colussi bakery near Campo Manin, adding salami and whatever else comes to hand, and a hip

The landing stage at Torcello.

flask charged with Poli grappa. May aim is to forsake bars and *bàcari* and head instead for the marshlands of Torcello, beyond the church of Santa Fosca and the cathedral of Santa Maria Assunta, past the latest archaeological excavations and the groups of tourists who hesitate by them, not knowing if they are allowed to venture further. In Guardi's day, we might have brought guns, either for a duck shoot from a slim, flat-bottomed *sandalo* in the waterways that criss-cross the marshland, or to sit in a hide made by sinking a huge wine barrel deep into the marsh, concealing the hunter from his quarry. I would have sat patiently on an upturned pail in this barrel, my head barely visible above the rim, biding my time, waiting for the fluttering shoals of birds to break cover. Hemingway liked to do this kind of thing. I prefer to tramp happily through the countryside with my dog, on a clear and windless autumn afternoon, our landscape painted in a rich but restrained palette of ochre and russet, enlivened by scatterings of rushes like silver needles, and the animated reflection of the pallid grey sky in pools and streams. It is extraordinary to think, as I sip my grappa in perfect solitude, that over a millennium ago this desolate place had a hugely profitable industry reclaiming salt from the lagoon, a population of some 20,000 people, and a busy port that dispatched and received goods from Constantinople and far beyond. Later, the water level rose dramatically and fatally, when the Po river repeatedly burst its banks. An immense body of dark silt, like a vengeful Leviathan, slouched its way towards the laboriously reclaimed land of Torcello, feeding and fertilising the hungry marshland until it fattened into a verdant feast for mosquitoes. Successive plagues of malaria steadily culled the population, until finally the city and its port were abandoned, the residents inevitably finding themselves drawn to the metropolitan sanctuary of Venice. Torcello's identity as a thriving trade centre and revered holy see was soon eroded in the Venetian myth-making process, so that to this day it is mostly seen as a mere ornamental outpost of the Republic.

Santa Maria Assunta, the cathedral of Torcello, a twelve-hundred-year-old fastness amid the marshes.

Returning to Santa Maria Assunta, Torcello's cathedral, one can marvel at the vast gold and blue *Madonna* in the apse, and at the so-called 'Doomsday Mosaic' on the west wall opposite, an early Byzantine *Last Judgement*, with Christ at its centre, smashing the stout locks of the gates of Hell, Satan lying defeated on the wreckage beneath. I suggest that a no less entrancing image, often overlooked, can be found in one of the small marble reliefs that decorate the pulpit. Though it dates from the 11th century, in spirit it is a relic of the pagan world that continued to infest the imagination of early Christians and whose iconography was routinely pillaged and put to use in creating a pictorial scheme for the new religion. An intriguing collage of such work makes up this building.

The relief in question depicts four figures. At the centre is wing-sandalled Kairos, the personification of the Opportune Moment, the instant so few of us manage to seize. To the left is a resolute young man who has grasped Kairos's forelock, niftily grabbing his chance; to the right, a visibly too-thoughtful youth clutches vainly at Kairos's shoulder: he has missed his moment. And behind this unlucky man stands sorrowful Metanoia, the personification of Repentance and Regret, mourning an infinite number of lost moments. Once fixed in the mind, this tableau may hold myriad meanings for many people. For me, it specifically serves as a reminder that Venice is—and always will be—full of Opportune Moments, all-too-easily missed in the hurly-burly of itineraries, the urgency that short stays in the city compel, the tidal waves of redundant and repetitive information that overwhelm us.

I hope that this collection will encourage visitors to drink and think their way around the lagoon city in a reflective and receptive mood, ever alive to the startling, beautiful and improbable insights and perceptions that Venice will always present.

The Bars and Cafés

Al Squero. Popular *bàcaro*, crowded in the early evening, overlooking a famous gondola repair yard. No. 9

Al Todaro. Long-established bar, café and ice cream shop in a prominent location on St Mark's Square. No. 10

Al Remer. Excellent restaurant in an ancient *palazzo*, with outdoor seating overlooking the Grand Canal. No. 18

Al Volto. Traditional Venetian *bàcaro*, serving drinks and snacks (*cicchetti*). Full meals also available. No. 21

Ba'Ghetto. Kosher restaurant with a charming outdoor garden and an excellent range of wines. No. 13

Blu Bar. Simple hole-in-the-wall bar-café. A useful pit-stop if you are visiting San Sebastiano. No. 7

Caffè Rosso. A popular stalwart on the lively Piazza Santa Margherita. Tiny old café with lots of outdoor seating. No. 23

Chioschetto. More than just a refreshment kiosk. They offer a good range of drinks, salads and sandwiches, as well as a beautiful view over the Giudecca Canal. No. 12

Da Filo. Lively and popular bar, where a diverse crowd spills out onto the street. No. 8

Excelsior. One of Venice's finest and most opulent hotels, with private beach huts and a well-known bar. No. 14

Florian. One of the most celebrated cafés in Venice, with a jewel-box interior and attentive waiters. On St Mark's Square. No. 19

Gritti Palace. Luxury hotel in a Grand Canal *palazzo*, with a glorious bar overlooking the water. No. 16

Harry's Bar. One of the most famous watering holes in Venice. Exemplary cocktails and unobtrusive service. No. 2

Il Mercante. Alternative cocktail bar serving innovative mixtures. No. 6

La Calcina. Excellent small hotel on the Zattere, with a restaurant and bar and delightful small cocktail snug. No. 17

Le Coccinelle. Very simple refreshment stand at Piazzale Roma. No. 25

Palazzetto Pisani. Secluded, elegant *palazzo*-hotel with a bar overlooking the Grand Canal. No. 11

Quadri. Famous café on St Mark's Square with an illustrious clientèle. No. 4

Redentore. Café, bar and *cicchetteria* overlooking a small canal. No. 24

Rosa Salva. Pastry shop and confectioner that also doubles as a bar and tea room. No. 20

Schiavi. Perhaps the most famous of the Venetian *bàcari*, serving wines by the glass and excellent *cicchetti*. No. 3

Sottovento. Tucked away in an inner courtyard on Murano, a pleasant café bar and simple restaurant. No. 22

TiME Social. Cocktail den in the old-fashioned manner. Good list of drinks, excellently prepared. No. 15

Trattoria San Basilio. Small, family-run restaurant on the Zattere serving home-made Venetian food and good regional wines. No. 1

Villa Laguna. Comfortable hotel on the Lido, overlooking Venice, with an excellent lounge bar on the waterfront. No. 5

The Drinks

Index

Contd from p. 4

Edited by Annabel Barber

Map by Dimap Bt. © Blue Guides
Line drawings by Gabriella Juhász © Blue Guides
Interior images: pp. 114, 139, 173: Wikimedia Commons CCO 1.0
All other images © Blue Guides

Prepared for press by Anikó Kuzmich

Grateful thanks from the editor and publisher to:
Wietske and Machiel Jansen Schoonhoven, Nellike Henneman

Author's acknowledgements
I owe much to the many people who in countless ways have encouraged
and inspired this project: Sofia Pellegrini Curtis and Jennifer Macmillan
of Palazzo Barbaro, Bikem and Roger de Montebello of Palazzo Contarini
Polignac, Maria Novella Papafava dei Carraresi of Galleria Itinerarte, and the
artists Geoffrey Humphries, Martino Sorteni and Ludovico De Luigi.
Others include Cristiana and Konstantin Akinsha, Cat Bauer, Eva and John
Birchall, Sandra Chinaglia, Arrigo Cipriani, Ambra Curato, Oleg de Baikoff,
Val de Furrentes, Valerio de Scarpis, Gregory Dowling, Alberto Franchetti,
Donata Grimani, Philip Gwynne-Jones, David Hewson, Katherine Kovesi,
Ivan Kuraev, Fabrizio Lazzarotto, Marco Loredan, Jeremy Magorian, Claudio
Manni, Irina and John Mappin, Natalia and Leonid Margolis, Christine
Marigonda, Daniela, Chris and Mara Mason, James O'Neill, Paul Pattinson,
John Francis Phillimore, Davide Rucati, Mikhail Sakharov, Vikram Seth,
Magdalina Skikun, Holly Snapp, Rick Stein, Isabel Trafton, Simon Waldron,
Leigh Warre and Christopher Wayman. I also thank Maria Pia and Marco
Balestra and their family, whose beautiful castle in Umbria serves as a perfect
writer's retreat. Warm thanks are also due to my editor and publisher,
Annabel Barber and Tom Howells. My greatest debt of all is to Katia Margolis
and her daughters Roxana, Alexandra and Ariadna—and our dog Spritz,
a cheerful and willing companion on many a 'drink and think' outing.